SAMURAI CASTLES

HISTORY | ARCHITECTURE | VISITORS' GUIDES

JENNIFER MITCHELHILL

PHOTOS BY DAVID GREEN

TUTTLE Publishing

Tokyo | Rutland, Vermont | Singapore

Contents

Preface

Just before the largest clash of samurai in Japanese history, at the Battle of Sekigahara in 1600, Chiyo, the wife of samurai Yamauchi Katsutoyo, wrote her husband a letter, concealing it in the chin strap of a messenger's hat.

The Battle of Sekigahara, fought between the two major powers, the Toyotomi and the Tokugawa, was to decide the fate of Japan for the next 268 years. The side on which a samurai chose to fight would determine his fate and that of his family for generations to come. The stakes were high and loyalties ran deep. To fight on the losing side meant loss of territory, loss of one's master and the life of a wandering, masterless samurai called *ronin*. Victory could have gone either way. It was finally determined by

the betrayal of a Toyotomi loyalist general who defected to the Tokugawa side in the midst of the battle.

Chiyo had received word of the potential betrayal. Her husband, Yamauchi, had served under the great sixteenth-century leader Oda Nobunaga and his successor, Toyotomi Hideyoshi. Her letter relayed vital information about Toyotomi forces and suggested her husband switch allegiance. Fortuitously, Katsutoyo took her advice and fought on the winning Tokugawa side. As a reward, he was made first lord of the province of Tosa on the island of Shikoku. With Chiyo, he constructed Kochi Castle, beginning the Yamauchi dynasty where 16 consecutive generations ruled Tosa over the following 268 years. In recognition of Chiyo's

efforts, today a bronze statue of Katsutoyo's wise wife watches over the approach to the main citadel.

Japanese castles are rich in stories of intrigue, sacrifice and betrayal. They stand as majestic monuments to the samurai who once ruled Japan.

Some 160,000 samurai fought in the battle of Sekigahara on October 21, 1600 to determine the supreme ruler of Japan. The Eastern Army led by Tokugawa Ieyasu, and the Western Army led by Ishidi Mitsunari, each comprised allied *daimyo* (feudal lords) from provinces all over Japan. The banners painted on this Japanese screen show the family crest of the 40 or so *daimyo*'s armies who took part in the battle. After a day of fighting and the loss of 40,000 lives, Tokugawa Ieyasu declared victory. Thus began the 268-year rule of Japan by the Tokugawa shogunate. (Late Edo era, 19th century. Collection of the City of Gifu Museum of History)

Introducing Japan's Samurai Castles

Japanese castles as we know them today were predominantly built in the late sixteenth century. This was a time when warriors introduced themselves before engaging in hand-to-hand combat, when honor could be restored by slicing open one's abdomen, and when great attention was paid to the rituals of the tea ceremony, poetry writing and dying.

Regional warlords had been fighting over territory from about 1470. By the mid-sixteenth century, a few were anxious to unify the country and secure absolute power. The central characters were larger than life and stories of their courage, skill and sheer audacity have entertained generations for over 400 years. Among them were Oda Nobunaga (1534–82), the ruthless youth who used courage and exceptional military skill to subdue enemies with armies five times the size of his; Toyotomi Hideyoshi (1536–98), the poor peasant boy who rose to rule the country; and Tokugawa Ieyasu (1542–1616), the shrewd warlord who worked quietly in the background, waiting patiently before taking control of the country.

One of the most imposing legacies of this period is the Japanese castle. During the scramble to unify the country, *daimyo* (lords of a domain) built castles to protect their territory and act as a base from which to rule their domain. Representative of a *daimyo*'s power and wealth, these grand fortresses were cunningly planned to confuse the enemy on their approach to the main keep. Should an attacking army successfully cross a moat and scale the outer stonewalls, numerous shooting holes and trapdoors allowed the besieged samurai to bring their weapons to

bear on those below. Constructed predominantly of wood, the vulnerable main buildings were adorned with symbols to ward off the enemy, fire and the elements.

Of the hundreds of castles built in the late sixteenth and early seventeenth century, only a handful have survived in their original condition. Hundreds were ordered to be demolished when the country was unified by Toyotomi Hideyoshi in 1582. Hundreds more were destroyed by the Tokugawa shogunate (military government) in 1615. The majority of the remaining 170 or so castles fell victim

Japanese castles were as much a symbol of power as a fortification. The multistoried main tower (*tenshu*), with its graceful arrangement of sweeping roofs, dominated the surrounding landscape. Usually sited on raised ground, the tower served both as a lookout and as a reminder of the lord's authority. (Hiroshima Castle)

to Imperial orders to destroy any trace of Japan's feudal past after the Meiji Restoration in 1868. Allied bombing during World War II razed seven of the 19 remaining main castle towers (*tenshu*), leaving countless subsidiary towers, stonewalls, gates and moats.

The 100 or so castle sites that can be visited today offer a fascinating glimpse into Japan's past. This book explains the historical background to Japanese castles, who built them and why. It describes their construction and their form. Finally, it presents 24 of the best surviving castles.

A History of the Japanese Castle

Long before the Japanese castle as we know it today took shape, simple fortifications were used as a defense against invading forces and internal warring factions. Their use is first recorded in the *Nihon Shoki* (Chronicles of Japan), written in the eighth century. The *Nihon Shoki* details the fight between two powerful court families, the Soga and the Mononobe, in AD 580. Their disagreement concerned Buddhism, introduced via Korea in 552. The Soga welcomed the new religion while the Mononobe saw it as a threat to their political influence.

Early defenses were primitive. The *Nihon Shoki* notes that the Soga built mansions surrounded by palisades and moats, whereas the Mononobe used bundles of rice plants (*inaka*) as protection against the arrows from enemy archers. Remains from these early fortifications can still be found throughout Japan.

In the mid-seventh century, the Japanese imperial court, which ruled from Yamato, near Nara, began pushing north into the Ezo territories in an attempt to expand the area under their control. (The Ezo are ancestors of the Ainu people in Hokkaido). Small palisades (*saku*) and stockades (*ki*) were built near Niigata in 647. The Ezo responded by building earthen ramparts and dry moats. The fortifications were called *chashi*, an Ainu word for castle.

Unrest along the Korean peninsula in the late seventh century sparked fears of an invasion from China. Rows of stones along the sides of small hills, which may have

formed walls, and an earth embankment intended for use as a protective dam, have been discovered in Kyushu, southern Japan. Stonewalls in valleys and the remains of observation towers have also been unearthed in the area.

Kamakura (1185–1333) and Muromachi (Ashikaga) (1338–1573)

In 794, the Imperial court moved from Nara to Heian-kyo, present-day Kyoto. Dissatisfaction with the Imperial court led to the establishment of a new military system of rule in 1185. The emperor remained in Kyoto as the spiritual and cultural leader of the country while the newly appointed shogun (hereditary military leader), Minamoto Yoritomo, set up his headquarters at Kamakura. Representatives were posted in each province to oversee tax collection. Following Yoritomo's death in 1199, his widow, Hojo Masako, took control of the shogunate as shikken (shogunal regent). Her family ruled for the next 134 years.

In 1266, and again in 1281, a new external threat arose when the Mongols attempted to invade Japan via north Kyushu. A stonewall was built around Hakata Bay in Fukuoka prefecture to help stave off the invaders. Adverse weather, however, proved the most effective defense, leaving Japan one of the only countries to not fall under Mongol rule.

Fending off the Mongol attacks severely depleted the resources of the Kamakura shogunate. There were no spoils of war, so there was little with which to reward the southern vassals for defending the coast. This contributed to a growing dissatisfaction with the ruling Hojo family and gave the then emperor, Go-Daigo, the justification needed to overthrow the Kamakura shogunate in 1333. Go-Daigo's aggression prompted Aso, a vassal of the Hojo family, to lay siege to the Imperial stronghold at Akasaka and attack the Chihaya fortress on Mount Kongo. These

The Siege of Osaka Castle. Although effectively becoming the most powerful *daimyo* after his victory at the Battle of Sekigahara in 1600, Tokugawa hegemony was not assured until Toyotomi Hideyoshi's heir, Hideyori, was disposed of. In the winter of 1614, then again in the summer of 1615, Tokugawa forces besieged Osaka Castle. This screen shows the Summer Battle of Osaka Castle in 1615. Over 5,000 samurai and 21 generals are depicted. One of the generals, Kuroda Nagamasa, took painters with him to the battle site to obtain an authentic rendition of events.

modest fortresses, using the height and contour of the mountains to their advantage, were little more than simple wooden stockades linking towers and gates.

Emperor Go-Daigo's reign was short-lived and he was exiled to the Oki Islands in the Sea of Japan. Three years later, in 1336, the shogunate was overthrown by one of its own generals, Ashikaga Takauji. Taking the title of shogun, Ashikaga established his headquarters at Muromachi, a suburb of Kyoto, to begin the 235-year reign of the Ashikaga shoguns (1333–1568). This was known as the Muromachi era.

The two centuries of Ashikaga rule were characterized by a cultural renaissance in literature and the arts, including the tea ceremony, *ikebana* (flower arranging) and landscape gardening. At the same time, Kyoto's central control began to weaken while civil disorder grew as provincial lords vied for land and power. Influential provincial families revolted against the heavy taxes imposed to fund extravagant shogunal expenditure centered around Kyoto. Religious bodies also exerted their growing power and peasants formed leagues (*ikki*) to rise up against the injustice of landlords and moneylenders. Ouchi Yoshihiro fortified the port town of Sakai, near present-day Osaka, with a ring of small towers or turrets as part of a plan to attack Shogun Yoshimitsu Ashikaga in 1399. Yoshihiro committed ritual suicide (*seppuku*) on the battlefield after his besieged rebel army was crushed the following year.

The Warring States Period (1477–1576)

The second century of the Muromachi period was beset by war. A disagreement between two powerful vassals over shogunal succession in 1467 sparked a bloody conflict in Kyoto. Eleven years of fighting, in what became known as the Onin Rebellion, devastated the capital city. Political stability broke down as provincial lords turned away from the central authority. Open warfare broke out. By the time hostilities ended in 1477, around 20 powerful warlords ruled their territories autonomously, with 200–300 lesser warlords subordinate to them. Changes in power were violent and frequent. Fighting continued amongst these lords and their ancestors over the next century. The emperor remained in Kyoto as a figurehead, alongside the seven Ashikaga shoguns appointed between 1490 and 1573.

Both the emperor and the shogun, however, held little authority outside of the capital, Kyoto.

This period is known as the Sengoku jidai or Warring States period (1477–1576). As rival warlords clashed to protect or increase their territory, thousands of simple fortifications in the form of wooden palisades and stone embankments were erected on mountains. These fortifications spread over the mountain, with the main citadel located at the highest and least accessible point. A network of satellite castles radiated from the main citadel, each protected by a small stronghold and guard posts. Baileys or enclosures were carved out of the mountains at different levels. Inside were fences, towers, stables, storehouses, walkways, bridges, gates and often a simple keep. Timber from the surrounding forests was the main building material. Stone was used to strengthen the base of gatehouses and towers and to prevent erosion from the excavated slopes.

These early mountain fortresses had the advantage of height for observation and protection but were difficult to supply and to deploy troops from. The warrior lord usually lived in a mansion at the foot of the mountain, which was sometimes surrounded by a moat or equipped with a watchtower. These mountain strongholds were the precursor to the earliest type of 'modern' castle. In the event of attack, the lord would retreat to the safety of his mountain fortress, though most battles were fought on open ground.

Late Warring States Period (1560s–70s)

Ambitious warlords in the second half of the sixteenth century formed alliances to overthrow the incumbent shogun, Ashikaga Yoshitaki. To do so, a warlord had to march his army to Kyoto to obtain the emperor's endorsement. One such warlord, holding territory close to Kyoto, was Oda Nobunaga. The location of Nobunaga's land at Owari, though small, gave him a distinct advantage over potential rivals such as Uesugi, Takeda or Mori, whose large holdings were further away. Their march to Kyoto was significantly more hazardous, passing through unfriendly territory as they left their own domains undefended for extended periods. For example, Imagawa Yoshimoto, a powerful warlord, and his 15,000-strong

Azuchi Castle, built by Oda Nobunaga in 1576, was the first modern castle. Situated on a hill on a main route close to the capital of Kyoto, it was easy to access. To withstand attack, it employed defenses on a scale not previously seen in Japanese castles. As a first line of defence, mansions (*yashiki*) belonging to Oda's top vassals lined the main route to the main tower. Barbican-style gateways (*masugatamon*), multiple enclosures, enormous stonewalls and hidden floors further strengthened the castle's defenses.

army were slaughtered as they attempted to pass through Nobunaga's domain in 1560. The surprise attack by Oda's small army of 3,000 on familiar territory gave them an advantage over the larger army.

Azuchi-Momoyama Period (1575–1600)

As warlords allied and became more powerful, their castles took on a greater role. As well as providing a vantage point and last line of defense, castles began to be used as administrative centers from which the warlords ruled their domain. They were constructed in more accessible locations, usually on a hill for vantage, and close to major routes to monitor who passed through their territory.

Local lords encouraged the growth of towns around their castles, the central position and size of the castles being a symbol of their power. Castles built on lower ground and close to major routes were more vulnerable to attack. Firearms had been introduced to Japan in 1543 and more elaborate defenses were needed to counter the new weapons. Castles needed to be larger and stronger.

Oda Nobunaga was the first to build such a castle. Between 1576 and 1579 he built an enormous castle at Azuchi, 31 miles (50 km) east of Kyoto. The first modern castle in Japan, it differed from the previous wooden forts in many ways. It was situated on a hill rather than a mountain, and was close to a main highway. A town was laid out at the base of the castle next to Lake Biwa and merchants were encouraged to settle there. This location gave Oda a strategic vantage point over the main road leading to the capital, Kyoto. It also facilitated the administration of surrounding areas, the supply of goods to the castle and the deployment of troops. However, it also made the castle easier to attack. Massive stonewalls were used to combat this threat, a feature that became characteristic of the Japanese castle. The main tower (Tenshu) of Azuchi Castle was seven stories high, where previously towers had been only two or three stories. Many smaller towers protected the main keep.

Azuchi Castle was as much a proclamation of Oda Nobunaga's power as it was a fortress. Colorful and ornately decorated, it was a flamboyant structure befitting the self-made military leader. Ultimately betrayed by one of his vassals in 1582, Oda Nobunaga was wounded. With little hope of escape, he committed ritual suicide. The Tenshu and other towers of Azuchi Castle were burnt down and were never rebuilt.

Oda's death paved the way for his general, Toyotomi Hideyoshi, to complete the unification of Japan. To consolidate and herald his new position, Toyotomi constructed even more impressive castles at Osaka and Momoyama (Fushimi Castle), plus a fortified palace called Jurakudai (Palace of Pleasure) in Kyoto. Contemporary European visitors described these castles as magnificent in terms of their size, strength and grandeur, unlike any buildings they had seen before.

The black Tenshu of Toyotomi's Osaka Castle was a feature of the later castles he ordered built at Hiroshima

Portrait of Tokugawa Ieyasu at the Battle of Nagakute, 1584, painted in the seventeenth century. (Collection of Tokugawa Art Museum. Photo Wikimedia Commons)

(1589), Okayama (1589) and Matsumoto (1590). These black castles stand in contrast to the Tokugawa castles, which were usually white. As Toyotomi was building his opulent castles, he decreed in his *Shirowari* policy of 1582 that only *daimyo* under his control could retain their castles. Thousands of mountain castles were subsequently destroyed or abandoned, depriving the rural gentry of a fortified base from which to stage an uprising. By 1583 there were 204 domains across Japan, each comprising a main castle and a number of smaller ones. Hideyoshi's power, however, was not yet secure. The four *daimyo* charged with distributing Nobunaga's estate and administering civil government opposed Hideyoshi's leadership. Their resistance led to the Battle of Shizugatake, near Lake Biwa, in 1583.

Victorious, Hideyoshi continued to consolidate his position as a new threat emerged, that of Tokugawa Ieyasu. The two met in battles at Komakiyama and Nagakute in Owari, in 1584. In the absence of a decisive victory, an agreement was reached in 1585 that awarded Ieyasu the former Hojo territories in the east—Izu and eight Kanto provinces, including Edo. In exchange, Ieyasu left his ancestral holdings closer to Kyoto, a departure that effectively removed him from the seat of power.

Hideyoshi, meanwhile, introduced a number of measures to secure his authority, which were to affect Japan's social structure and the maintenance of peace over the next 300 years. The *Taiko Kenchi* (Land Survey) from 1583 to 1598 recorded the dimensions and yield of every ricefield in Japan. Hideyoshi sought to make the main rice cultivator a permanent tenant, responsible for paying the tax on his land. In this way, he now controlled the farmers, who made up 80 percent of the population, by tying them to the land and obliging them to deliver tax in the form of rice. The ration was usually *niko ichimin*— 'two to the prince and one to the people.' Land holdings were described in *koku*, the amount of rice they produced (1 *koku* weighs 300 lb/150 kg). A land grant by Hideyoshi (or Tokugawa Ieyasu after

Three Great Unifiers of Japan

If a bird won't sing:
Nobunaga would say: "Kill it"
Hideyoshi would say: "Make it want to"
Ieyasu would say: "Wait"

Toyotomi Hideyoshi

Three great men led Japan out of its 100 years of war during the latter half of the sixteenth century: Oda Nobunaga (1534–82), Toyotomi Hideyoshi (1536–98) and Tokugawa Ieyasu (1542–1616).

Oda Nobunaga began the process of unifying Japan following his victory at the Battle of Okehazama in 1560. His motto to 'Rule the Empire by force' was imposed on conquered territories through strict laws and punishment. Nobunaga's success was due to his innovative, often brutal battle tactics, sound judgment and consolidation of military victories with civil administration. Some of his more famous battles were the capture of Inabayama Castle (1567), the Mt Hiei Massacre (1571) and the Battle of Nagashino (1575). Deceived and attacked by one of his vassals, Oda Nobunaga committed *seppuku* in 1582. Before his death, Oda had brought about one-third of Japan under his rule. He was succeeded by Toyotomi Hideyoshi, who completed the unification of Japan by offering generous peace terms to powerful families such as the Mori of the western provinces and by defeating or persuading other enemies to unite. By 1590 he had completely subdued the territorial warlords, uniting Japan as the head of a powerful *daimyo* alliance.

Unlike Nobunaga or Ieyasu, who both came from influential warrior families, Toyotomi Hideyoshi came from humble peasant stock. He rose from the lowly

Oda Nobunaga

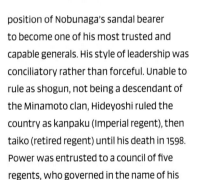

Tokugawa Ieyasu

position of Nobunaga's sandal bearer to become one of his most trusted and capable generals. His style of leadership was conciliatory rather than forceful. Unable to rule as shogun, not being a descendant of the Minamoto clan, Hideyoshi ruled the country as kanpaku (Imperial regent), then taiko (retired regent) until his death in 1598. Power was entrusted to a council of five regents, who governed in the name of his seven-year-old son Hideyori.

One of these regents, Tokugawa Ieyasu, assumed control of Japan in 1600 before being appointed shogun by the emperor three years later. Ieyasu was the wealthiest *daimyo*, ruling eight provinces in the productive Kanto area, with annual revenue of 2.5 million *koku*. He was, however, still threatened by the Toyotomi House so long as Hideyoshi's son and heir

lived. In 1615, he eliminated this danger by attacking Osaka Castle and causing Hideyori's demise. Ieyasu was an excellent general with a loyal following, as well as a talented administrator. Rather than fight Hideyoshi for the right to rule after Nobunaga's death, Ieyasu concentrated on strengthening his own territories, waiting for an opportunity to seize power himself. He lived for 13 years after becoming shogun, establishing a strong administration and consolidating his family's power base for the Tokugawa family to govern Japan for the next 268 years.

It is a common saying in Japan that Ieyasu ate the pie that Nobunaga made and Hideyoshi baked.

1600) was given in terms of *koku,* as was a *daimyo*'s revenue.

Hideyoshi's 'Sword Hunt' of 1588 aimed to ensure peace by disarming the general population. Peasants were instructed to hand over armor and weapons. Only samurai were allowed to possess and carry a sword. The large class of samurai farmers was forced to choose between soldiering and farming. Samurai were also encouraged to move to the castle towns, where they received a stipend in rice from their lord. Finally, in 1590 Hideyoshi issued an edict that effectively froze the social structure. The four classes of samurai, peasants, artisans and merchants were given separate legal identities. Samurai were prohibited from returning to their villages or changing lords and peasants were bound to the land and banned from entering trades or commerce.

The Battle of Sekigahara (1600) and the Siege of Osaka Castle (1615)

After Toyotomi Hideyoshi's death in 1598, a council comprising the five wealthiest *daimyo*—Tokugawa Ieyasu, Maeda Toshiie, Uesugi Kagekatsu, Mori Terumoto and Ukita Hideie—was appointed to rule until Hideyoshi's heir, Hideyori, came of age. This arrangement, however, soon broke down after Tokugawa and one of Hideyoshi's vassals, Ishida Mitsunari, vied for control.

A confrontation ensued at Sekigahara, about 25 miles (40 km) northwest of Nagoya, on October 21, 1600. The opponents, *daimyo* loyal to the Toyotomi house and those loyal to Tokugawa Ieyasu, were evenly matched, with around 80,000 men in each camp. The landmark battle brought together the largest number of warring samurai in Japanese history. In a decision that was to have major repercussions, 8,000 warriors from the Toyotomi side switched sides during the fighting. This surprise betrayal, led by Koboyakawa Hideaki, an adopted son of Hideyoshi, secured victory for Tokugawa Ieyasu.

Although Ieyasu now controlled the country, threats to his leadership remained. As a safeguard, he constructed a number of enormous, strategically located castles to keep his enemies in check. As Toyotomi had done, Tokugawa drew upon the resources of recalcitrant *daimyo* in his building campaign. By occupying their time and draining

their wealth, disgruntled *daimyo* were less able to raise a hostile army. Some of Japan's most impressive castles, including Himeji (1601–09), Hikone (1602–22), Nagoya (1610–28) and Edo (1593–1636), were built at this time.

Although Ieyasu became shogun in 1603, the supreme military ruler of Japan, there was still the threat of an uprising against his shogunate by *daimyo* who had not supported him at Sekigahara. These *daimyo* had been either stripped of their land or given much smaller territories. The possibility of a rebellion remained while Hideyoshi's heir, Hideyori, was still alive.

Ieyasu struck first. In 1614, with Hideyori in adulthood, he attacked Osaka Castle. On the flimsy pretext of an offending inscription by Hideyori on a bell, Ieyasu demanded that Hideyori leave Osaka Castle for a lesser fortress. Hideyori refused and enlisted the support of some 60,000 *ronin,* or masterless samurai, displaced after Ieyasu's confiscation of their *daimyo*'s land. Ieyasu besieged the castle during the winter of 1614–15 before a truce was negotiated, calling for Osaka Castle's outer defenses to be demolished. Ieyasu's army departed after the outer and middle moats were filled in and the outer walls pulled down. Hideyori, however, rebuilt the massive perimeter walls, compelling Ieyasu to again besiege the castle in the summer of 1615. After a failed counter-attack at Tennoji, Hideyori unsuccessfully sallied from the castle with a small force. Withdrawing inside the castle, the Tenshu now ablaze from artillery fire, he committed *seppuku.* The last major uprising against Tokugawa rule had ended, leaving the shogunate unchallenged for the next 250 years.

The Edo Era (1615–1867)

Prior to the Edo era, around 100 major castles were built between 1576 and 1615 in the grand style of Azuchi, Osaka and Fushimi. Significant castles and their related towns, including Himeji, Kanazawa, Wakayama, Kochi, Hiroshima, Edo, Okayama, Kofu, Sendai, Kumamoto, Hikone, Yonezawa, Shizuoka and Nagoya, all came into being during these years. But many of the largest castles were built in the early Edo era, with prominent family members of the Tokugawa installed in the most important, including Himeji (1601), Nagoya (1610) and Osaka (1620). *Tozama*

The Reshuffle of Territories
After the Battle of Sekigahara

After Tokugawa Ieyasu's victory at the Battle of Sekigahara in 1600, *daimyo* were rewarded or punished according to whether they had supported or opposed him.

Yamauchi Katsutoyo, having earlier served under Nobunaga and Hideyoshi, was advised to align with Ieyasu before Sekigahara. In recognition of his support, he was awarded the province of Tosa, where he built Kochi Castle. This province was taken from Chosokabe Motochika, who supported the Totyotomi side. Hideyoshi's adopted son, Ukita Hidiie, was stripped of his three provinces, including Okayama Castle, in favor of Kobayakawa Hideaki, Hideyoshi's foster son, who switched sides at Sekigahara. Kobayakawa's treachery helped pave the way for Tokugawa's victory. Mori Terumoto, a powerful *daimyo* from the western provinces, sided with the Toyotomi loyalists, and despite not engaging in the battle was severely punished. Mori's vast holdings were reduced from 1,205,000 *koku* to 369,000 *koku* and his castle at Hiroshima given to Fukushima Masanori. The castigated *daimyo* was sent to the remote town of Hagi on Japan's southwest coast, far from his traditional power base and even further from Edo, the new center of power.

Ii Naomasu, a Tokugawa vassal, had the honor of being the first into battle. The lead position had been granted to Fukushima Masanori, but Ii, a long-time loyal follower of Tokugawa, believed he should lead rather than Fukushima, who had been one of Toyotomi Hideyoshi closest vassals. Ii argued that since he was escorting Tokugawa's fourth son, he should inspect the front lines. In this way, he was first into battle. Both men were well rewarded. Ii was given Omi province, where he built a castle at Hikone, and Fukushima was given Mori Terumoto's Bizen provinces and castle at Hiroshima.

Himeji's strategic location as the gateway to the western provinces, home to many Toyotomi supporters, was given to Tokugawa Ieyasu's son in law, Ikeda Terumasa. Ikeda had distinguished himself in the lead-up to Sekigahara by seizing Gifu Castle.

Maeda Toshie was one of five regents appointed by Toyotomi Hideyoshi to care for his young son, Hideyori, but died a year after Toyotomi in 1599. Maeda had been a trusted friend and vassal to Toyotomi but his two sons were divided in their loyalty. One son, Toshimasa, championed Toyotomi at Sekigahara and was consequently divested of his provinces. These were given to his brother, Toshinaga, who had supported Tokugawa. Toshinaga then became the wealthiest *daimyo* after Tokugawa, holding Kanazawa Castle and receiving an annual income of 1,250,000 *koku*.

Bloody scenes from the Battle of Sekigahara, 1600. Warriors in red belonged to Ii Naomasu's army, whose red-lacquered armor earned them the nickname 'Ii's Red Devils.' Battles were a chance for samurai and *daimyo* to distinguish themselves for further advancement. Rewards were usually in the form of increased territory and income. Once a samurai had land that produced 10,000 *koku* of rice per year, he was awarded *daimyo* status.

daimyo (outside lords) were compelled by the Tokugawa shogunate to contribute to the building of these castles on the pretext of national defense. However, with the country relatively stable, this act served to further deplete their resources and prevent insurrection.

Castle building virtually ceased after the threat from the Toyotomi house was eliminated in 1615. A new law, *Ikkoku ichijo rei*, or one castle per province, forced *daimyo* to demolish all castles in their domains with the exception of their primary residence. Within a matter of years, some 400 castles were torn down. Across the country, about 170 castles remained, a number that stayed relatively constant over the following centuries.

The construction of new castles, or repairs to existing ones, required approval by the Tokugawa shogunate. If the *tenshu* burnt down, as they often did through lightning strikes or accidents, they were not usually rebuilt. Castles built in this peaceful period typically had few defensive features. The *tenshu* was obsolete. The *daimyo* and his family lived in a residence in one of the secondary compounds, with the main buildings now used for administration. Often finished in white plaster with decorative horizontal bands, the castles of this period tended to be less ornate than the earlier ones of the Azuchi-Momoyama era.

The Meiji Period (1867–1912) and the Boshin War (1868–69)

Japan's isolation from the West ended after the American Commodore Mathew Perry's fleet arrived in Japan in 1853 and demanded that Japan open its doors to Western trade. Many Japanese were dissatisfied with the unfair trade treaties that followed. An alliance of samurai from the western domains of Chosu, Satsuma and Tosa, together with Imperial court officials, pressured Shogun Tokugawa Yoshinobu to pass political power over to the 15-year-old Emperor Meiji. This Yoshinobu did quite peacefully, although widespread unrest, violence in Edo and an Imperial decree to abolish the Tokugawa house prompted him to launch a failed campaign against the newly installed emperor. Together with those loyal to Tokugawa, Yoshinobu retreated to northern Honshu, and later to Hokkaido, where he founded the Ezo Republic. This last

rebellious faction was finally defeated at the Battle of Hakodate at Fort Goryokaku in April, 1869. Japan in its entirety now came under Imperial rule.

The Meiji Restoration returned political power to the emperor after nearly 700 years of military rule (*bakufu*) by three shogunates: Kamakura (1185–1333), Muromachi (1333–1568) and Tokugawa (1603–1868). Edo, renamed Tokyo (eastern capital), became the national capital. By 1871 the shogun's domains were rationalized and converted into 47 prefectures. *Daimyo* were replaced by government appointed officials to manage them. Castles were now an unwelcome reminder of Japan's feudal past, and in 1873 an order was given to reduce their number. The majority were destroyed over the next two years, leaving only 19 *tenshu* and numerous stonewalls and moats that were too difficult to dismantle.

World War II and Beyond

Seven of the *tenshu* that survived the Meiji Restoration were devastated by the Allied bombing campaign of World War II: Nagoya, Hiroshima, Wakayama, Okayama, Fukuyama, Ogaki and Gifu. Several towers remaining at Osaka Castle were also lost. Although Himeji city was bombed extensively on July 3, 1945, the castle miraculously survived.

A renewed interest in castles developed in the early to mid-twentieth century. New *tenshu* were reconstructed in concrete at the Osaka, Nagoya, Wakayama, Hiroshima, Kumamoto, Okayama, Odawara and Fukuyama castle sites. Reinforced concrete, which was thought to be stronger than traditional building materials—stone, wood, mud, plaster and tile—was cheaper and easier to work. However, it was discovered that the original materials were more suited to the Japanese climate. Recent reconstructions using traditional materials are helping to keep alive the specialized skills needed to build a castle. Now recognized for their historical value, unique architecture and romantic association with the samurai, Japanese castles are increasingly popular tourist destinations. Several are listed as UNESCO World Heritage Sites, including Nijo and Himeji castles on the main island of Honshu, and Nakajin, Nakagusuku and Shuri castles on the southern islands of Okinawa.

The Design of a Japanese Castle

The Japanese castle reached its developmental peak during the early seventeenth century. The power struggle between the Toyotomi and Tokugawa camps during the Momoyama period (1575–1600) stimulated the construction of hundreds of castles. The enormous quantity of materials and manpower needed for these increasingly complex fortresses were supplied by local farmers, merchants and samurai, as stipulated by their *daimyo*. Massive castles such as Osaka, Edo and Nagoya required substantial contributions from *daimyo* throughout the country. Remarkably, these major castles were completed in a matter of years. This frenetic period of castle building lasted 40 years, beginning in 1575 with Oda Nobunaga's revolutionary Azuchi Castle and ending in 1615 with the Tokugawa's edict banning new castle construction.

Initially a defensive stronghold, the castle became more of an administrative center and expression of power as Japan's political situation began to stabilize in the early seventeenth century. Towns grew up around the castle and industries evolved to serve the needs of the castle population.

Viewed from a distance, a Japanese castle appears to be little more than a large tower crowned with layers of sweeping roofs. This tower, however, is just one part of a castle complex made up of minor towers, storehouses, gates and a palace set in compounds delineated by earthworks, stonewalls, plastered mud walls and moats. Each castle is unique, distinguished by its location, whether sited on a mountain, hill or plain; its layout; the kind of stones used in its walls; the style, size, defensive and decorative detail of its main tower; the position, number and style of its other towers and gates; and whether it had a palace, gardens and other administrative buildings.

Optimal Siting

The optimal location for a castle changed with the political situation. Mountain castles (*yamajiro*) were common during the Warring States period (1467–1568), with thousands of warrior lords fighting for territory. It is estimated that around 5,000 of these simple fortifications were erected. Natural obstacles such as cliffs, rocky terrain and forests provided additional protection for these wooden forts. Although their inaccessibility hindered attack, mountain castles were susceptible to siege, difficult to build and inconvenient as an administrative base.

With the consolidation of territories into the hands of a few powerful warlords in the second half of the sixteenth century, it was advantageous for castles to be built close to major transport routes for easy access and to monitor

Yamajiro

Hirayamajiro

Hirajiro

Ukishiro

the movements of other warlords. Castles needed to be accessible both as a barracks and for administrative purposes. They were built either on top of a hill surrounded by a plain (*hirayamajiro*) or on a flat area of land (*hirajiro*). Since low ground offered less protection, many castles were built close to the sea, a lake or a river, with water diverted to fill surrounding moats. Many of the large modern castles built between 1596 and 1615, such as Himeji Castle, were *hirayamajiro*. Castles built on flat land surrounded by wet moats were called 'floating castles' (*ukishiro*) or 'water castles' (*mizujiro*).

Layout

Japanese castles comprise a series of compounds with the main tower (*tenshu*) situated in the highest, innermost bailey or enclosure (*honmaru*). Subsidiary enclosures housed the lord's residence, storehouses and retainers' quarters. These were commonly called *ninomaru* (second enclosure), *sannomaru* (third enclosure) and *nishinomaru* (western enclosure). Individual enclosures were separated by earthworks, stonewalls and moats. A castle may have only a few enclosures or as many as seven, such as at Kanazawa Castle. The layout (*nawabari*) of these enclosures was crucial for a castle's defense. The aim was to confuse an enemy and obstruct access to the main tower.

Natural topography was maximized in castle building. A hill site presented opportunities for a layout with minimum excavation, while natural features, such as a river or a steep escarpment, were often incorporated into the castle's defensive system. The perimeter of the castle was usually circular or pentagonal, as these shapes reduced blind spots and required fewer soldiers to defend them. Extensive castle grounds kept vulnerable wooden buildings out of enemy range. The grounds of Edo Castle, for example, stretched 3 miles (5 km) from east to west and about 2.5 miles (4 km) north to south.

There were four types of layout: *doshinen*, *hashigokaku*, *renkaku* and complex. A *doshinen* layout had the main enclosure at the center with the second and third enclosures arranged in concentric rings around it. Osaka Castle was one of the few castles to adopt this form because of the extensive earthworks needed to form the encircling moats. A second type of layout, *hashigokaku*, placed the main enclosure at the apex of a hill from which the second and third enclosures descend like steps. Inuyama Castle is typical of this style. A *renkaku* layout placed the main enclosure in the center with the second and third on either side, as at Nagoya and Hikone castles. A more complex layout can be seen at Himeji Castle where the approach to the main *tenshu* twists and turns before descending into the inner enclosure through a series of gates and small courtyards. Such a layout confused intruders, forcing them to slow down to the advantage of the defending samurai.

Stonewalls

Towering stonewalls (*ishigaki*) are one of the most imposing legacies of the Japanese castle. Reaching as high as 98 ft (30 m), these dry stonewalls have survived more than 400 years of rain, earthquakes and war. Their existence today is a tribute to the great skill of the Japanese stonemason.

There were two main types of stonewall: a stone-faced embankment and a free-standing wall. Stone-faced walls

Doshinen

Hashigokaku

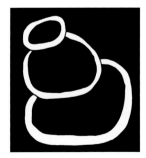

Renkaku

Complex

surrounded castle enclosures and could reach heights of up to 98 ft (30 m). Stones were piled against a hill that had been carved to a desired angle, or against an embankment formed from a moat excavation. Free-standing walls were much lower and used as the base for towers, gates and mud walls. Behind the outer stone face was an inner core filled with pebbles and earth.

Various kinds of stones were used in castle walls: field stones, cut stones, cracked stones and pebbles. Enormous single stones (*kagami*) were positioned at important entrances to impress visitors, such as the Higo stone at Osaka Castle and the Kiyomasu stone at Nagoya Castle. Auspiciously shaped stones were also placed at important entrances. Representing water, the hexagonal tortoise stone at the rear gate of Kanazawa Castle 'protects' the castle from fire.

The availability of suitable stones, the financial resources of the lord and the timeframe determined the types of stone utilized. Specially cut stones took longer to prepare and were more costly than locally gathered field stones. Consequently, field stones and roughly hewn stones were the most common, with finely cut or decorative stones reserved for corners, important gateways and the base of the main tower.

No mortar was used in the stonewalls. This allowed the walls to move slightly during Japan's frequent earthquakes, minimizing damage to the wall and the wooden structure above. The skill in stonewall building lay in positioning individual stones to lock them together. The earliest stonewalls were constructed with rough stones stacked against an earth embankment: random stone piling (*ransekizumi*) or field stone piling (*nozurazumi*). *Gobozumi* was a more sophisticated form of random style piling where long rectangular stones were embedded deep into the earth to stabilize a wall. 'Beaten and inserted masonry' (*uchikomi-hagi*) was the most common type of piling. It used individual rocks roughly hewn into shape by hammer and chisel. As these stones were still quite rough and asymmetrical, cracked stones and pebbles were used to fill any gaps in the outer face. Cut and inserted masonry (*kirikomihagi*) was the most technically advanced form of stone piling. Precisely hewn stones were carefully aligned to create a wall without gaps. The specially shaped stones were either square, rectangular or hexagonal and laid

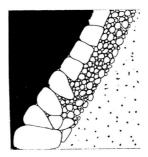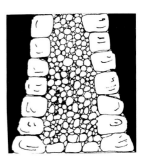

Above left A stone-faced embankment showing the base stone (*ne ishi*), piling (*gobozumi*) at the lower part of the wall and upper part (*uchiko-mihagi*). Between the large outer stones and the earth embankment is a layer of pebbles, which facilitate drainage. (This diagram is for illustrative purposes only as a wall would usually only employ one kind of piling.)

Above right A free-standing wall.

evenly in rows (*nunozumi*) or at right angles (*kaginote*). Particular attention was paid to the corners of stonewalls, with larger rectangular stones piled alternately in a zipper-like fashion (*sangizumi*).

Stonewalls were originally low and vertical. If the ground was soft or the building heavy, they were built on an incline to create a wider, more stable base. The more refined the piling, the steeper a wall could be. As walls became higher and the buildings they supported larger, walls were built in a parabolic shape. The curve in the wall was achieved using wedge-shaped stones. The smaller end of the stone faced outwards, the larger inwards. Curvature of the wall lessened the strain on the lower stones by distributing the weight over a wider area.

Narrow steps on the inside of the castle wall provided access to the top of the walls. Steps running along the length of a wall (*gangi*) enabled a number of warriors to

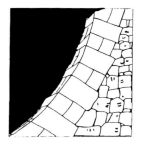

Ransekizumi and *nozurazumi* (field or random stone piling).

Uchikomihagi and *sangizumi* (corner stone piling).

Kirikomihagi (cut and inserted masonry).

The fan-shaped stonewalls of Osaka Castle reach up to 79 ft (24 m). These types of walls are a feature of the strategically important castles at Nagoya and Himeji built during the early years of Tokugawa rule when there was still the threat of rebellion from supporters of the Toyotomi House.

ascend the wall rapidly to defend the castle. Such steps can be seen at Wakayama, Hagi and Osaka castles.

Moats

Moats (*hori*) surrounding castle enclosures provided further protection for the *tenshu*. Those filled with water or fine mud were usually fed naturally by the water table or by diverting water from a nearby source.

The size of a moat depended upon whether it was an exterior, interior or surrounding moat. The exterior moat was usually the widest and deepest, up to 26 ft (8 m) deep and 85 ft (26 m) wide. The sides were often faced with stone to prevent erosion and followed two basic forms, the U shape (*yagenbori*) and the box shape (*hakobori*).

Walls

Low walls (*hei*) encircled castle enclosures, delineating areas and linking towers and gateways. Set atop stonewalls and interspersed with shooting holes, these walls protected samurai defending the castle. They blocked the view into and across the castle grounds and directed the approach to the *tenshu*. Himeji Castle's labyrinth-like layout is

Yagenbori

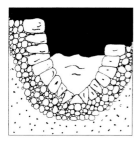

Hakobori

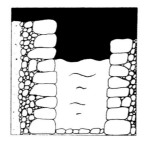

created by low walls acting as outdoor passageways.

The most common and simplest type of wall is a mud wall (*dobei*). Approximately 6.5 ft (2 m) high, it consists of a timber and bamboo frame covered in a mixture of mud and straw. Although occasionally left natural, the walls were usually plastered for greater strength and durability. Timber planks were sometimes added to line the walls, as at Matsuyama and Matsue castles. Alternatively, tiles were used to reinforce a wall and reduce the threat of fire, such as at Kanazawa Castle. A small tiled roof protected the wall from the elements.

Variations in walls included the soil wall (*tsujibei*), double wall (*nijubei*) and drum wall (*taikobei*), the latter so-named because the sides bulged out like a *taiko* drum. These particular walls were constructed by filling a wooden framework with compacted sand and clay, stones or broken tiles and then covered with mud and plaster. They were stronger than *dobei* but also more time consuming to construct and too thick to contain shooting holes. Nijo Castle has an impressive 10 ft (3 m)-high *tsujibei* running beside the Ninomaru Palace.

CASTLE BUILDINGS

Towers, gates, storehouses and the lord's living quarters made up a castle's buildings. The centerpiece was the large main tower or keep (*tenshu*).

Main Tower

The *tenshu* was an elaborate structure used as a lookout, storage facility and, in some cases, accommodation. As the heart of the complex, it was situated inside the innermost enclosure (*honmaru*) at the highest point in the castle grounds. Being the last line of defense, it was the most heavily protected of all the buildings.

There are two styles of *tenshu*: lookout style (*borogata*) and multilevel style (*sotogata*). Early *tenshu* were usually constructed in the *borogata* style. These ornate two- or three-story wooden buildings were crowned with a watchtower. Maruoka, Inuyama, Hikone and Matuse castles are all examples of this type. The square upper story watchtower was incorporated into the middle of a lower level *irimoya*-style gabled roof. In contrast, a *sotogata tenshu* had multiple levels of the same shape that successively decreased in size as they rose skyward. Marugame, Hirosaki, Nagoya and Matsumoto castles are all examples of this style. The *sotogata* style was easier to construct than the *borogata* and was thus cheaper and quicker to build.

As a stronghold, the *tenshu* employed a number of defensive features. The building's height provided a commanding view over the surrounding area while multiple roof layers concealed the true number of internal levels, thereby confusing a potential invader and giving defenders an opportunity to hide or escape. Shooting holes and stone-dropping windows aided defence while slatted windows prevented objects being flung inside.

As well as a defensive structure designed to impress or discourage an enemy, a *tenshu*'s sheer size, roofing arrangement, window shape, color and decorative roof tiles symbolized power and wealth. *Tenshu* were at least three stories high, their size being commensurate with the power of the *daimyo*. Yet size was not essential to convey power. Architectural beauty was also important, with some of the most striking *tenshu* relatively small, like those at Hikone, Inuyama and Uwajima. This aesthetic grandeur was achieved by a combination of layering upsweeping roofs and a complex arrangement of roof gables.

There are two types of roof: *irimoya* and *kirizuma*. The *irimoya* roof is a two-sided roof with a closed triangular gable at opposite ends. The *kirizuma* roof is simply two sides joined at the top. This type of roof often covers the pillars of a post-and-beam gate. The triangular gable (*hafu*) can take the form of an *irimoyahafu*, *chidorihafu* or *karahafu*. The sides of the *irimoyahafu* extend to the edges of the roof. The smaller *chidorihafu* appear to be attached to the roof, with the sides joined at an angle to the roof. The *karahafu* is an undulating roof.

On the main *tenshu* of Matsumoto Castle, the top roof gable is an *irimoyahafu*, the middle undulating gable a *karahafu* and the lower gable a *chidorihafu*.

Borogata-style *tenshu*: Hikone Castle (**left**), Gifu Castle (**center**) and Inuyama Castle (**right**).

Sotogata-style *tenshu*: Matsumoto Castle (**left**) and Hirosaki Castle (**right**).

The two lower triangular gables on the *tenshu* at Hirosaki Castle are *kirizumahafu*. They cover the protruding stone-dropping windows but are not attached to the roof. The top gable is an *irimoyahafu*, its sides extending to the edge of the roof to form a closed triangular gable.

Although windows (*mado*) were necessary for light and for defense of a castle, their arrangement and form also contributed to the *tenshu*'s external beauty. Three main types of window were used: push out timber windows (*renjimado*), latticed bay windows (*degoshimado*) and bell-shaped windows (*katomado*). *Shoji* and timber sliding screens were used to secure windows from the inside.

Japanese *tenshu* were finished in black lacquered timber, white plaster or a combination of both. Castles built before 1600, when Toyotomi Hideyoshi was in power—Azuchi (1576–79), Maruoka (1576), Osaka (1583), Okayama (1589–97), Matsumoto (1590–1614), Hiroshima (1589–99) and Kumamoto (1601–07)—were often black. Those built by the Tokugawa shogunate and its supporters after 1600—Himeji (1601–09), Hikone (1602–22), Nagoya (1610–28) and the reconstructed Osaka (1620–29)—were often white. This is thought to be either a sign of support (black for Toyotomi and white for Tokugawa) or due to available resources, as plastering was more expensive. Alternatively, how a castle was finished may have been in line with the development of castle technology. The exposed timber framework, flooring and walls of the earlier castles were susceptible to fire. Walls were made stronger, weatherproof and fireproof in later castles by covering a bamboo lattice with mud and straw upon which 1 inch (3 cm) of plaster made from a mixture of slaked lime, shell ash, hemp fiber and seaweed was applied. Exterior plastered walls were sometimes lined with wooden planks or tiles to protect them from the elements and provide further strength.

Gold decoration and various symbolic features embellished the *tenshu*. Stone, bronze or gilded mythical dolphin-like creatures (*shachihoko*) acted as 'protective' roof ornaments, while gargoyle-like tiles on the eave corners (*onigawara*) warded off bad spirits. Rows of roof end tiles displayed the *daimyo*'s crest. The overall effect of Japanese castle *tenshu* was one of restrained opulence.

Early *tenshu,* such as those at Maruoka and Uwajima castles, usually stood alone as a single tower. Others, such as at Hikone and Matsue castles, were attached to a subsidiary tower. The *tenshu* of larger castles, such as at Nagoya and Kumamoto, were connected by a crossing or connecting tower (*watariyagura*). Himeji, Wakayama and Matsuyama castles have a compound *tenshu* arrangement whereby the main keep is connected to multiple smaller towers by *watariyagura* or an extended one-story tower (*tamonyagura*) to create a small courtyard or to encircle the entire inner enclosure.

TENSHU DETAILS

Roofs

Layers of sweeping tiled roofs are unique to Japanese castles. Tiles were usually made of clay but could also be made from stone, lead or copper. Although structurally unnecessary, roof gables proliferate on Japanese castles, adding a graceful upswept roof.

Tenshu Types

Below, left to right *dokuritsushiki* (independent), *fukugoshiki* (attached), *teiritsushiki* (connected), *renketsushiki* (compound).

  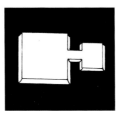 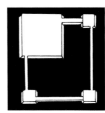 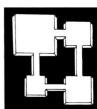

Left Matsue Castle has an attached-style (*fukugoshiki*) *tenshu*. Access to the five-story tower is through a heavily fortified two-story annex.

Below Himeji Castle has a compound tower arrangement (*renketsushiki*). The main five-story *tenshu* is connected to three smaller *tenshu* by corridors forming an internal courtyard. In the event of an attack, defenders could retreat to one of the subsidiary towers.

Defensive Openings

Decorative Gables

A round plaster-covered shooting hole overlooking the entrance to Osaka Castle enabled defenders to fire upon intruders approaching the main gate.

***Shachihoko* (dolphin-like tile)**

Placed on either end of a roof ridge, *shachihoko* are mythical creatures combining a tiger's head with the body of a fish. The raised tail symbolized the creature throwing up waves and causing rain to fall. Made of wood, stone, tile, bronze or gilded, it was a charm to guard against fire and ward off disaster.

***Nokimarugawara* (round eave end tiles)**

Lining the edge of the roof eaves, these round tiles displayed the family crest of the lord or carried a design symbolizing water—lightning and fire being an ever-present danger to the predominantly wooden buildings.

***Nokihiragawara* (flat eave end tiles)**

A decorative flat tile lining the roof edge between the round eave end tiles.

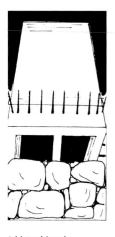

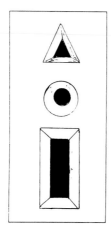

Roof end tile

***Onigawara* (gargoyle-like 'monster' tile)**

This fierce-looking tile positioned at the apex of the roof also helped 'protect' a castle. Tiles in this position often incorporated the lord's family crest in the design as well as waves and clouds to symbolize water, fire being one of the greatest threats to the castle.

Gengyo

Decoration at the apex of a gable to conceal the tip of the ridge beam and rafters.

Ishiotoshimado (stone-dropping window)

These openings were incorporated into stone, mud or wooden walls and towers. Small trapdoors and removable floorboards allowed defenders to hurl stones, boiling water or hot sand upon invaders trying to scale a castle wall.

***Sama* (shooting holes)**

Shooting holes were rectangular for arrows and square, triangular or circular for guns. Larger on the inside, the telescoped opening allowed a weapon to be freely maneuvered while minimizing a defender's exposure to enemy fire.

Turrets

Towers or turrets (*yagura*) formed a vital part of a castle's defensive system. Acting both as a watchtower and a point from which to fire on an attacking enemy, they were strategically placed above gateways and at the vulnerable corners of stonewalls, which were the easiest part of the wall to scale.

Originally used to store weapons (*ya* means arrow, *kura*, storehouse), castle towers served as storage: *teppoyagura* (gun tower), *hatayagura* (flag tower), *shioyagura* (salt tower); as the place from where the signal drum (*taiko-yagura*) was sounded; and as a turret from which to view the moon (*tsukimiyagura*). Towers were commonly identified according to their compass location and corresponding zodiac sign. A northwest tower, for example, was called *ushitorayagura* (ox/boar tower), a southeast tower, *tatsumiyagura* (dragon tower), a southwest tower, *hitsujisaruyagura* (sheep/monkey tower) and a northwest tower, *inuiyagura* (dog tower).

Towers were usually one level (*hirayagura*), two levels (*nijuyagura*) or three levels (*sanjuyagura*). Different types

A *nijuyagura* (two-story tower) with stone-dropping windows acts as a watchtower over the moat and main entrance to Osaka castle. The tower in the foreground is a *yaguramon* (tower gate) which makes up part of the main gate into the castle grounds.

included corner towers (*sumiyagura*), long towers (*tamonyagura*), connecting or crossing towers (*watari-yagura*) and gate towers (*yaguramon*). A *tamonyagura* was a covered gallery from which a line of soldiers could fire through shooting holes. These towers, such as at Hikone and Himeji castles, were also used for storage and servants' quarters. *Watariyagura* provided a passage between the main and minor *tenshu*. Himeji, Iyo Matsuyama and Matsumoto all use *watariyagura* in this way.

Hirayagura

Nijuyagura (two-level corner tower)

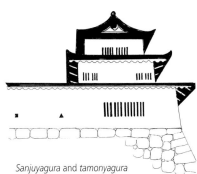

Sanjuyagura and *tamonyagura* (three-level tower and corridor tower at left)

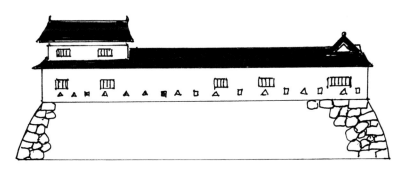

Tamonyagura and *nijuyagura* (corridor tower and two-level tower at left)

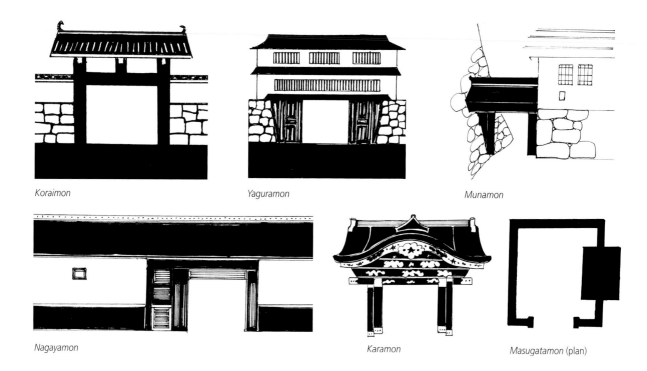

Koraimon

Yaguramon

Munamon

Nagayamon

Karamon

Masugatamon (plan)

Gates

Gateways (*mon*) were the most vulnerable part of a castle. Heavily reinforced gates were fashioned from wood or a combination of wood, stone and plastered mud walls. Wooden gates in important positions were usually reinforced with intricately decorated ironwork, which not only strengthened the gate but proclaimed the importance of the lord.

Of the many kinds of gates, the most common were the *koraimon* and *yaguramon*. A *koraimon* is a post-and-beam gate with a roof extending over the front posts and gate, plus two subsidiary roofs over the rear supports. A simpler form is the *yakuimon*, which has one roof covering the entire gate. A *yaguramon* is a two-story gatehouse with an opening on the ground floor and a guardhouse with firing positions on the first floor. It was either free-standing or positioned between two stonewalls.

Koraimon were usually positioned at significant entrances in conjunction with a *yaguramon* to form a box-shaped gate (*masugatamon*), so-named after the *masu* or rectangular-shaped rice container. This style of gate was used at important entrances to the castle. A *koraimon* formed the first gate with the much larger *yaguramon* set

A free-standing *yaguramon* at Hirosaki Castle. The absence of walls beside the timber-and-plaster structure indicates that this castle was constructed in a relatively peaceful period, alleviating the need for major defensive structures to protect the *tenshu* in the inner enclosure.

at right angles to it. Passing through the first gate, visitors entered a courtyard enclosed by stonewalls topped with low mud or wooden walls lined with shooting holes. Trapped in the courtyard, enemies could be fired upon from all sides. This type of gate arrangement prevented outsiders from seeing straight into the castle.

Important south-facing front gates were usually called *otemon*. Secondary gates were called *sakuramon* and north-facing rear gates were often referred to as *karamete*. Gates closest to the *tenshu* were usually smaller in order to restrict the passage of invaders, such as the *munamon* and *uzumimon* found at Himeij Castle. *Munamon* were post-and-beam gates wedged between two stonewalls, while an *uzumimon* was a small opening in a stonewall. Other castle gate types included the *karamon*, a post-and-beam gate with a cusped gable, and *nagayamon*, a gate set into a long storehouse or tenement building.

Other buildings within castle grounds included storehouses (*kura*) and *nagaya* (samurai quarters or tenements). Guardhouses (*bansho*) were positioned near main gates and manned by a contingent of samurai.

Palaces and Mansions

Early mountain castles were primarily a defensive stronghold with the lord's mansion (*yashiki*) situated at the base of the mountain. Castles built in the last quarter of the sixteenth century initially incorporated living quarters within the *tenshu*, such as at Azuchi Castle (1576). Over time, however, the relatively uncomfortable *tenshu* was abandoned in favour of a *yashiki* or a palace (*goten*) in an adjacent enclosure, usually the second enclosure (*ninomaru*). As well as the lord's residence, *goten* were used for ceremonial and administrative activities.

Goten (palaces) were single-story timber buildings set within gardens, usually in a secondary enclosure (*ninomaru*). The lord and his family would live in the palace rather than the *tenshu* (main castle tower). Sliding screens enabled the size and configuration of rooms to be changed by the opening, closing or removal of a screen. Screens were solid and were either made of timber or paper, translucent or latticed. (Kawagoegoten.)

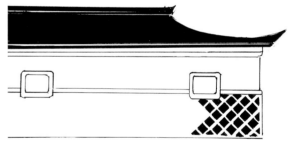

Kura

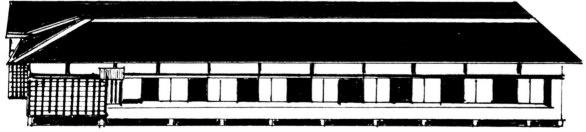

Goten

Below The wooden rain doors (*amado*) at Kawagoegoten can be removed leaving the wooden-floored hallway (*engawa*) open to the courtyard. White *shoji* (translucent paper sliding screens) slide in tracks to open or close the inner rooms to the exterior. The structure rests on timber posts to allow airflow, keeping the building cool in the humid Japanese summer. The overhanging eaves direct heavy rain away from the timber building and into the gravel-filled drainage pit running the length of the building.

Top The intricate lattice windows at the entrance to Kawagoegoten allow inhabitants a protected view to the outside.

Above Sumptuous paintings on gold leaf adorn the *fusuma* (solid paper sliding screens) at the Omote Shoin of Nagoyagoten. Tigers and pine trees were common themes in reception rooms, symbolizing power, strength and longevity.

Built in the Shoin style, *goten* were single-story timber buildings often with a staggered plan. Sliding timber or layered paper doors (*fusuma*) and transparent paper doors (*shoji*) opened between rooms and out onto gardens. The floors of the living areas were covered with straw mats (*tatami*) while a timber-floored hallway (*engawa*) ran between the matted rooms and the exterior sliding doors. Shoin-style buildings had an audience hall (*ohiroma*) with a desk alcove (*tsukeshoin*), display area (*tokonoma*) and staggered shelving (*chigaidana*). The *ohiroma* was the most opulent reception room, with gilded walls painted with scenes of tigers, pine trees, birds and bamboo. The most important individual was always seated with his back to the *tokonoma*. Floor levels denoted rank, with the lord (*daimyo*) occupying the highest level (*jodan*) during an audience. His guests or retainers sat either in the middle level (*chudan*) or lowest level (*gedan*) according to their rank. Guards stationed behind a wall of the *jodan* were on constant alert to protect the lord.

Construction Techniques

Various types of timber were used in castle construction. Cypress (*hinoki*) was prized due to its strength, absence of knots, softness and ease of working. Zelkova (*keyaki*) and fir (*mominoki*) were alternatives. Precisely cut joints, in preference to nails, joined the framework together. This allowed for movement in the event of an earthquake and expansion and contraction in the course of Japan's seasons.

Foundation Stones

Foundation stones were laid out at intervals on a compacted earth base (*tenshudai*) to support the timber posts of the *tenshu* frame. The raised earth base was faced with stones.

Foundation stones of the original *tenshu* of Okayama Castle. To compensate for the uneven surfaces of the stones, timber posts were fashioned to stand solid on each stone, creating a level base upon which the timber *tenshu* was built.

Wooden Joints

Ancient temple construction techniques were applied to castles. Intricate joints allowed for expansion, contraction and movement during earthquakes and changes in weather. Later castles had a central pillar that ran from the ground to the top story for further stability.

Walls

The exposed timber floors, posts and walls of the early castles, such as Maruoka, were susceptible to fire. Later castles, such as Himeji, fireproofed their walls by covering a bamboo lattice and straw frame with consecutive layers of a mud and straw mixture. The mud wall was then plastered and sometimes tiled or covered with timber planks for additional protection.

Framework

Although standard measurements are used in Japanese architecture that allow components to be prepared before assembly, carpenters still had to make alterations on site. An example would be a stonewall base that was not perfectly square, or uneven foundation stones.

Left The multiple layers of a castle wall. Covering the bamboo lattice are four layers of mud and two layers of plaster and tiles. (Kanazawa Castle)

Right A bamboo lattice bound with straw before being covered in layers of mud.

Castle Builders: Samurai and Daimyo

The modern Japanese castles presented in this book were built by *daimyo* in the late sixteenth century. *Daimyo* were lords of the samurai and vassals of the shogun, the supreme military ruler.

Samurai were military gentry educated and trained in martial arts, horsemanship and cultural pursuits. Meaning 'one who serves,' samurai lived according to a strict ethical code of bravery, integrity and loyalty. Fierce warriors, they would fight to the death in order to protect their lord and his property. Samurai would vie for the honor of being first into battle, stating their name and ancestry before engaging in combat. They would willingly undertake ritual suicide (*seppuku* or *hara-kiri*) to restore their honor, to atone for a mis-demeanor or to thwart an enemy from taking their head. Along with honing their military skills, samurai pursued the finer arts of poetry, the tea ceremony and calligraphy, and during the peaceful Edo era (1603–1868) took on administrative roles in their lord's domain.

Samurai belonged to an elite class, ranked above farmers, artisans and merchants. They were accorded the right to carry a sword, wear colors forbidden to the lower classes and install a gated entrance to their residence. The Meiji Restoration in 1868 heralded the demise of the samurai. Since the elite warrior class was incompatible with the new democratic ideals being put in place, it was dissolved between 1873 and 1876. The centuries-old feudal military system was abolished and a Western-style government was introduced with the emperor installed as head of state.

Daimyo were lords of the samurai. Meaning 'great name,' *daimyo* controlled

land with an annual income of at least 10,000 *koku*. One *koku* was equivalent to about 300 lb (150 kg) of rice, the amount needed to feed one man for a year. Land was acquired from being appointed to oversee it by the shogun during the Kamakura (1185–1333) or Muromachi (1368–1573) eras or through military gain in the Warring States period (1477–1576). *Daimyo* built castle towns in their domain to supervise the surrounding villages. They were permitted to run their domains freely in regard to taxation, law enforcement and the maintenance of an army. In return, the shogun expected their loyalty and military or national service as required. During the Edo era (1600–1868), *daimyo* were required to take up residence in Edo every alternate year through the *Sankin kotai* (alternate residence) system. A *daimyo*'s wife and eldest son would remain in Edo when they returned to their domains. Such rules discouraged plots against the shogun and depleted a *daimyo*'s resources. Rivals of the Tokugawa were almost impoverished from financing the gigantic castles of Edo, Sumpu, Osaka, Nagoya and Nijo. Finally, the 1615 law for military houses (*Buke sho hatto*) forbade *daimyo* to move troops outside their own domains, to form political alliances with other *daimyo*, to maintain more than one castle in their domain or to marry without shogunal approval.

The shogun was the most powerful *daimyo* or supreme military leader. The three main shogunates throughout Japan's history were the Kamakura, Muromachi

A *daimyo* inspects the head of a defeated enemy. As samurai were rewarded for performance in a battle, the presentation of enemy heads provided proof of their success.

and Tokugawa. The castles presented here were built just prior to and at the beginning of the Tokugawa shogunate.

Who occupied which castle and where was determined by the *daimyo*'s relationship to the supreme leader or shogun. Oda Nobunaga awarded castles and territories to his vassals in reward for their service from 1560 until his death in 1582. His successor, Toyotomi Hideyoshi, did likewise, but with a greater number of territorial lords under his control who had been subdued rather than allied, he reshuffled his territories to remove potential rivals far from the political center of Kyoto. For example, he moved Tokugawa Ieyasu to the distant, and much larger Hojo provinces in the east of Japan, and stationed his most trusted vassals in the west where dissent was most likely to occur. After the Battle of Sekigahara in 1600, Tokugawa assigned territories and castles according to whether a *daimyo* had supported or opposed him. Faithful *daimyo* became *fudai*, entrusted with land in central Japan. Although small, these domains were strategically located on the Kanto plain, in the Kinai district or bordering a powerful enemy's territory. In all, there were about 176 *fudai* lords, 130 of whom provided the shogunate with councilors and senior officials during the Tokugawa era.

Those lords who had not supported Tokugawa at Sekigahara were either stripped of their land or had their holdings severely reduced. Known as *tozama daimyo* (outside lords), they were usually from the west or north of Japan. Having received their *daimyo* status from either Oda Nobunaga or Toyotomi Hideyoshi, they were considered untrustworthy

Above Samurai of the Chosu clan inspect a map during the Boshin War in the 1860s. Western influence is evident in the military uniforms worn by the samurai at the rear. Western hairstyles, however, had not yet been taken up, with samurai still favouring the traditional topknot style. (Western ships arrived in Japan in 1853, marking the beginning of the end for the 268 years of military rule by the Tokugawa shogunate.)

Left A samurai carried two swords (*daisho*). The larger one (*katana*) was the standard fighting sword, while the short sword (*wakizashi*) was used for fighting at close quarters, to behead a defeated opponent or to commit ritual suicide (*seppuku*). While samurai armor was functional, helmets were often individualized with designs symbolizing speed and agility, such as the dragonfly or rabbit. *Daimyo* often had extravagant attachments on their helmets, such as gilded horns, antlers or a golden crescent moon or, like Toyotomi Hideyoshi, a huge sunburst crest.

and were thus prevented from occupying senior positions in the shogunate. There were 86 *tozama daimyo* in 1600.

Besides *fudai* and *tozama* domains, there were also *shimpan* domains run by *daimyo* related to the Tokugawa through either birth or adoption. These trustworthy lords were given territories closest to the shogunal territory. *Sanke* domains were held by *daimyo* born into the three houses directly descended from Tokugawa

Ieyasu, who could provide successors to the Tokugawa shogun. These domains were Owari, Kii and Mito. *Tenryo* (heavenly) domains were held specifically by the shogunate and comprised 25 percent of Japan.

Castles rarely changed hands once the political situation stabilized in the mid-seventeenth century. Most remained within the same family until the Meiji Restoration in 1868.

VISITING JAPAN'S
FINEST CASTLES

FUKUYAMA CASTLE
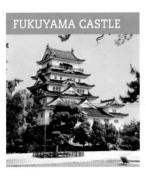

WAKAYAMA CASTLE
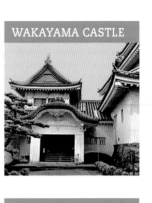

KOCHI CASTLE

IYO MATSUYAYA CASTLE
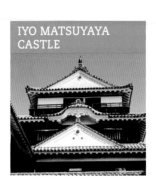

HIMEJI CASTLE
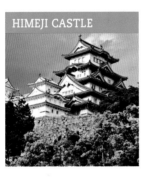

HIROSHIMA CASTLE
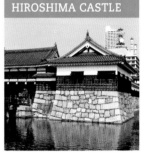

NIJO CASTLE
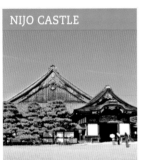

BITCHU-MATSUYAMA CASTLE
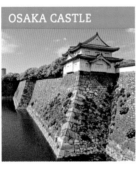

OSAKA CASTLE

KANAZAWA CASTLE

OKAYAMA CASTLE
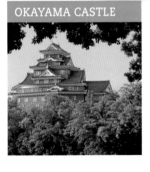

MATSUE CASTLE
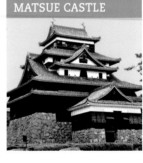

HAGI CASTLE
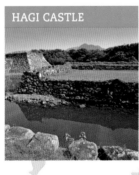

KUMAMOTO CASTLE
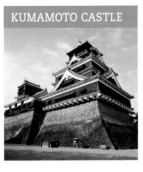

Kanaz
Daishoj
Fukui
Maruoka
Sabae
Fukuchiyama
Tottori Izushi Miyazu
Matsue Takeda Obama
Hirose Tsuyama Sasayama Tanabe Zeze Hi
Katsuyama Tanba Kameyama Nijo Azu
Hamada Bitchu Tatsuno Himeji Takatsuki Kyoto
Matsuyama Sanda Osaka Nagas
Tsuwano Fukuyama Okayama Ako Akashi Yodo Is
Hagi Hiroshima Amagasaki Osaka Kan
Iwakuni Hiroshima Mihara Kishiwada Yamato
Fuchu Marugame Koriyama
Kokura Tokuyama Takatori
Fukuoka Akizuki Nakatsu Imabari Wakayama
Fukuoka Kizuki Tokushima Tanabe Shing
Hirado Karatsu Hiji Iyo Matsuyama
Saga Kurume Ozu Kochi
Omura Yanagawa Oita Uwajima
Nagasaki Usuki
Fukue Kumamoto Saeki
Shimabara Oka Nobeoka
Hitoyoshi
Takanabe
Sadohara
Kagoshima Obi

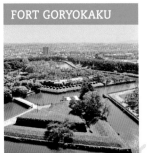
FORT GORYOKAKU

Color Key to the Castle Diagrams

■ Original building, including reconstructions prior to the 20th century
■ Authentic 21st century reconstruction using traditional materials and construction methods
■ Concrete reconstruction
■ Site of structure
■ Enclosure
▦ Moat

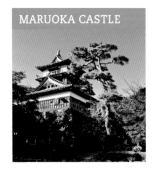
MARUOKA CASTLE

HIROSAKI CASTLE

TAKEDA CASTLE

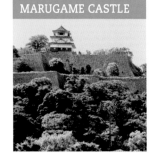
MARUGAME CASTLE

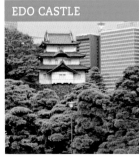

EDO CASTLE

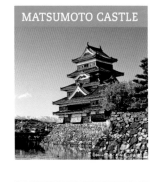
MATSUMOTO CASTLE

Goryokaku
Matsumae ⚑ 	Hakodate

⚑●Aoyama
Hirosaki 	⚑Hachinohe

⚑Kubota

⚑Morioka
Honjo ⚑

⚑Matsumine
Tsuruoka ⚑ 	⚑Shinjo
Murakami ⚑ 	Yamagata 	Sendai
	⚑Kaminoyama 	●Sendai
Shibata ⚑ 	Yonesawa ⚑ 	Fukushima
Yoita ⚑ ⚑Muramatsu 	⚑Soma Nakamura
Nagaoka ⚑ 	⚑Nihonmatsu
	⚑ 	⚑Miharu
	Aizu Wakamatsu
⚑Takada 	⚑Shirakawa
⚑Iiyama 	Otahara ⚑ ⚑Taira
Toyama 	Matsushiro 	Shimodate ⚑⚑Tanakura ⚑Izumi
	Utsunomiya ⚑ 	⚑Matsuoka
⚑Komoro Numata 	Mibu ⚑ 	Kasama
ama 	 	⚑Yuki 	⚑Mito
sumoto ⚑ Ueda 	Tokyo
iman 	⚑Takashima 	⚑Tsuchiura
⚑Takato
uyama 	⚑Naegi 	Kofu 	Edo ⚑ 	⚑Sakura
ya ⚑ Lida 	Odawara 	Kururi
Iwamura 	Numazu 	Sanuki ⚑⚑
agoya 	⚑Sumpu 	Otaki
ya ⚑Okazaki 	⚑Tanaka
a ⚑Yoshida ⚑Kakegawa
Hamamatsu Yokosuka

TAKEDA CASTLE

EDO CASTLE

NAGOYA CASTLE

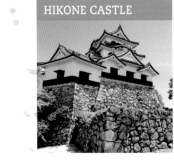
HIKONE CASTLE

NAGOYA CASTLE

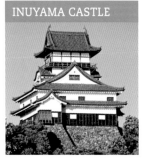
INUYAMA CASTLE

N

100 km
40 miles

Japan

Kumamoto Castle 1601–1607

With its sheer stonewalls, original buildings and extensive grounds, Kumamoto Castle is one of Japan's most impressive. Erected by the renowned castle builder Kato Kiyomasa (1562–1611) between 1601 and 1607, the immense castle originally contained 2 main towers (*tenshu*), 49 subsidiary towers, 18 tower gates and 29 castle gates. It covered an area of 242 acres (98 ha) and had a circumference of 6 miles (9 km). Sited on Mt Chausu, over-looking the town of Kumamoto, the castle was protected by rivers to the west and south.

Kato Kiyomasa was a trusted vassal and close friend of Toyotomi Hide-yoshi. In 1588, he was awarded half of the wealthy Higo domain following Hideyoshi's subjugation of the powerful Shimazu clan of Kyushu.

After Toyotomi Hideyoshi's death in 1598, Kato supported Tokugawa Ieyasu at the Battle of Sekigahara. This was due to his hatred of Ishida Mitsunari, who led the western army, rather than loyalty to the Tokugawa side. For his support, Ieyasu never-theless awarded Kato the other half of the province of Higo, increasing his revenue from 250,000 to 540,000 *koku*. With the permission of Tokugawa Ieyasu, Kato began construction of a castle in 1601. On its completion in 1607, the stronghold and surrounding town took the name Kumamoto.

Although Kato received rewards and favors from the Tokugawa shogunate, he remained loyal to his old friend Toyotomi Hideyoshi, vowing to protect his son and heir, Toyotomi Hideyori. After escorting

Below left Hohoatemon, the main gate of Kumamoto Castle, is so-called because it resembles a samurai's facial armor (*hahaote*). The gate frames the Tenshu in the background just as a *hahaote* frames a samurai's face.

Below The heavy timber door at the main entrance to the main tower (Daitenshu) has bars through which to view and shoot, and a small subsidiary entrance enabling the door to stay shut when under threat.

Opposite below Niyonoishigaki (stonewall of two styles). Advances in stonewall building are evident in these two walls. The more gently sloping wall to the right dates from the original construction in 1601. The steeper, more refined wall on the left was a later extension. Castle building techniques developed rapidly in the late sixteenth and early seventeenth century as *daimyo* scrambled for territory. When the Tokugawa gained complete control in 1615 after Toyotomi Hideyori had been deposed, new castle building virtually ceased.

Below Iidamarugokaiyagura, the five-story tower in the Iidamaru (Iida or enclosure), overlooks the Bizenbori (Bizen moat). Named after Iida Kakubei, who was in charge of the tower's original construction, it was reconstructed using traditional materials and methods in 2005. The Iidamaru is one of a series of lower enclosures that must be passed through to reach the Honmaru (main enclosure) where the Tenshu are located. The approach to the Honmaru is surrounded by sheer stonewalls, which twist and turn in order to block any views into the castle interior, designed to confuse a would-be attacker.

Hideyori to meet Ieyasu at Nijo Castle in 1611, Kato became suddenly ill and died of suspected poisoning. The domain was passed to his son, Kato Tadahiro, after which it was passed to the Hosokawa clan, in 1632. Eleven generations of the Hosokawa clan governed Kumamoto for the next 239 years until the Meiji Restoration in 1868.

In 1877, disaffected warriors led by the Satsuma clan from southern Kyushu, rebelled against the new Imperial Meiji government. This included a 50-day siege of Kumamoto Castle by government forces that drove the famed warlord Saigo Takamori and his forces out of the prefecture. The two main *tenshu* and many towers and gates within the castle grounds were burnt down during the siege.

LARGE AND SMALL CASTLE TOWERS (DAITENSHU AND KOTENSHU)

The six-story main Tenshu (Daitenshu) is connected to a smaller four-story Tenshu (Kotenshu). The first floor overhangs the stone base, allowing the floorboards to be lifted up and stones thrown down onto attackers. The original Tenshu of Kumamoto Castle was destroyed in 1877 during samurai uprisings against the newly restored Imperial government. The current Tenshu is a 1960 concrete reconstruction.

The large Tenshu rises 96.8 ft (29.5 m) above the stone base. The small Tenshu is 62 ft (19 m) high. The large Tenshu has three layers on the exterior and inside are six stories and a basement. The fish-like ornament (*shachihoko*) on the roof ridge is 4 ft (1.2 m) high. The small Tenshu has two layers on the outside, four stories inside and a basement. Both Tenshu were reconstructed in concrete in 1960.

Left and below The entrance to the Daitenshu and Kotenshu is heavily fortified with shooting holes, stone-dropping windows and spikes. The small doorway slowed down an attacking army, giving defenders ample opportunity to fire.

Above Originally completed in 1610 by Kato Kiyomasu, the Honmarugoten (palace) at Kumamoto Castle consisted of multiple rooms used by the lord for administrative and ceremonial duties. The palace included a living room, reception room and kitchen. Burnt down in 1877 during the Seinan Civil War, 25 of the original 53 rooms have been recently restored.

The lord received guests in the richly decorated Shokun (reception room). Wall murals on gold leaf illustrate tales from the Chinese Imperial court, believed to be the influence of Kato Kiyomasu. The ceiling of lacquered squares is decorated with gold leaf and intricate paintings of various plants. Samurai were stationed behind the rear painted doors to protect the lord.

POINTS OF INTEREST

The sheer stonewalls of Kumamoto Castle are called Mushagaeshi ('repelling warriors') because of their acute angle and strength.

Stretching 830 ft (253 m) in length, the plastered mud wall extending along the front of the Tsuboi River is the longest castle wall in Japan. Named Nagabei, meaning 'long wall', it was vital to the defense of the castle's southern perimeter.

Thirteen original buildings remain at Kumamoto Castle: Utoyagura (yagura means tower or turret), Gokenyagura, Hiramon, Akazuno-mon, Kita juhachikenyagura, Higashi juhachikenyagura, Gennoshinyagura, Yonkenyagura, Juyonkenyagura, Shichikenyagura, Tagoyagura,

Above The Ohiroma (main hall) of the Honmarugotten is made up of four smaller adjoining rooms: Tsuru, Ume, Sakura and Kiri. A corridor (*engawa*) from Tsuru hall leads to Wakamatsu hall, Shokun hall and the *sukiya*-style tearoom.

Left Kumamoto Castle is surrounded by 850,000 sq ft (79,000 sq m) of enormous, sheer stonewalls. In 2017, an earthquake damaged about 30 percent of the walls and a further 10 percent completely collapsed. To repair them, numbers are allocated to each stone removed so it can be replaced in exactly the same spot. Repairs to the 400-year-old walls will take about 20 years. The concrete Tenshu (Inuiyagura) behind, reconstructed in 1960, was severely damaged in the same earthquake and will also undergo restoration.

Left The multistory Utoyagura, with the Kotenshu and Daitenshu in the background, dates back to the original construction of Kumamoto Castle in 1601. With five stories and a basement, the size of this tower is indicative of the massive scale of Kumamoto Castle, this one tower alone being comparable in size to the main tower (*tenshu*) of many other castles. Kumamoto Castle originally had many multistory turrets like this one.

Nagabei and Kenmotsuyagura. The Iidamaru, Gokaiyagura and Honmarugoten (palace) are authentic reconstructions.

The Honmaru palace was constructed over two stonewalls, creating a dark basement passage known as Kuragari Tsuro ('passage of darkness'). This passage is unique to Kumamoto Castle.

Within the extensive park-like castle grounds are 17 of the original 120 wells, together with lawns and about 800 cherry trees.

Hosokawa Tadaoki was one of the favourite disciples of the famous Japanese tea master, Sen no Rikyu (1522–91). After retiring, Tadaoki renamed himself Sansai Soryu. The name Hosakawa Sansai is widely associated with Japan's historical tea culture. A replica of a unique long tearoom is in the Honmarugoten.

DIRECTIONS

Kumamoto Castle is located in the center of Kumamoto City, a 15 minute tram ride from JR Kumamoto Station. To walk from Kumamoto Station takes 30–40 minutes.

Color key on page 37

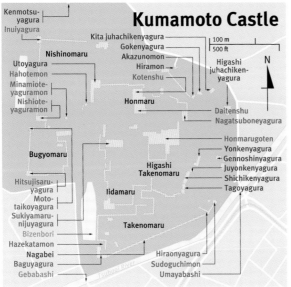

Kumamoto Castle

Kenmotsu-yagura
Inuiyagura
Kita juhachikenyagura
Gokenyagura
Akazunomon
Hiramon
Higashi juhachiken-yagura
Nishinomaru
Utoyagura
Hahotemon
Kotenshu
Minamiote-yaguramon
Nishiote-yaguramon
Honmaru
100 m
500 ft
N
Daitenshu
Nagatsuboneyagura
Honmarugoten
Yonkenyagura
Gennoshinyagura
Bugyomaru
Juyonkenyagura
Higashi Takenomaru
Shichikenyagura
Tagoyagura
Hitsujisaru-yagura
Moto-taikoyagura
Iidamaru
Sukiyamaru-nijuyagura
Bizenbori
Takenomaru
Hazekatamon
Nagabei
Hiraonyagura
Baguyagura
Sudoguchimon
Gebabashi
Umayabashi
Tsuboi River

Location Kumamoto, Kumamoto prefecture
Nickname Ginnan
Site area 242 acres (98 ha)
Type Hirayamajiro
Layout Renkaku
Tenshu type Borogata, Teiritsushiki (Connected)
Family crest Kato, Hosokawa

Kumamoto

Himeji Castle 1580, 1601–1609, 1617

Nicknamed the White Egret, Himeji Castle soars above the town of Himeji. Known today for its awe-inspiring size and ninja-defying layout, the castle once held the significant responsibility of guarding the gateway between the western and eastern provinces of Japan.

Located on the Sanyo Highway 80 miles (130 km) west of Kyoto, the strategic importance of this site is reflected in its rich history. First used as a stronghold in 1333 by Akamatsu Norimura, the governor of Harima province, it was taken by Kuroda Shigetaka on the orders of the Kodera family in 1545. Kuroda's son, Yoshitaka, also known as Kuroda Kanbei, was Toyotomi Hideyoshi's chief military advisor. He gave the fortress over to Hideyoshi to use as his base during the campaign to subdue the western warlords (*daimyo*) from 1577 to 1582. Hideyoshi raised a three-story main tower (*tenshu*) on the site in 1580. Hideyoshi's younger brother, Hidenaga, ruled Himeji after Toyotomi left to complete the unification of Japan from his base at Osaka in 1583. From 1585 Kinsoshita Iesada assumed control of the domain.

Following the Battle of Sekigahara in 1600, the victorious Tokugawa needed a base from which to monitor the western *daimyo*. Mostly *tozama daimyo* (outside lords who had not supported Tokugawa Ieyasu at Sekigahara), these *daimyo* were considered untrustworthy and were never allowed to enter the inner circle of the Tokugawa government. It was the *tozama daimyo* who ultimately helped remove the shogunate in 1867 and restore the emperor as ruler of Japan.

Ikeda Terumasa, a son-in-law of Tokugawa Ieyasu, began construction of a new castle in 1601. The Tokugawa shogunate assisted by ordering the western *daimyo* to support the project.

Far left One of eleven *shachihoko* on the roof ridges at Himeji Castle. The mythical creature has the head of a tiger and the body of a fish. The raised tail symbolizes the creature throwing up water as 'protection' against fire.

Above The magnificent Tenshu of Himeji Castle is a complex arrangement of four towers connected by corridors. Himeji Castle was one of the largest and most heavily fortified castles in Japan during the Tokugawa shogunate or Edo era (1603–1868).

Their vast resources and the use of the latest castle building techniques made Himeji one of the largest and most heavily fortified castles in Japan. Only the most loyal, experienced and healthy retainers were stationed at the castle. As such, the lord of Himeji castle changed frequently, with 31 different lords in charge throughout the Tokugawa reign between 1603 and 1868.

Honda Tadamasa succeeded the Ikeda family in 1617. His major engineering works included the addition of the western and third enclosures (Nishinomaru and Sannomaru). The Matsudaira and Sakakibara clans followed the Hondas before Sakai Tadazumi became lord of the castle in 1749. Sakai's descendants remained at Himeji Castle for the next 120 years until the Meiji Restoration.

Remarkably, given its location, the castle was never attacked.

After 1868 Himeji became a military city with infantry stationed on the castle grounds. Barracks replaced many of the early castle buildings. The remaining buildings, including the Tenshu, survived the bombing of the city during World War II. The castle is now listed as a UNESCO World Cultural Heritage Site.

POINTS OF INTEREST

Himeji Castle has a large Tenshu connected to three smaller Tenshu by corridors that form an enclosed courtyard. This is the most complex style of Tenshu arrangement. The large Tenshu appears to have five stories externally but actually comprises six stories and a basement. Two large pillars (*toshibashira*), nearly 3.3 ft (1 m) in diameter, reinforce the main Tenshu. They rise 82 ft (25 m) meters from the basement to the beam of the fifth floor, greatly increasing the building's strength. Four supplementary pillars extend from the four corners of the building for extra stability.

Firearms were stored on racks lining the Tenshu's internal walls.

Stone-dropping windows were built into the 20 in (50 cm)-thick walls. Samurai could wait in warrior hiding sites (*mushakakushi*) on each corner of the third floor of the main Tenshu to ambush intruders. Hidden shooting holes also lined the walls. The castle was designed to be self-sufficient during a siege. Rice and salt were stored in the basement, which also contained a well, and in a long storehouse called the Koshi kuruwa, located behind the main tower. The storehouse's northerly aspect helped to keep provisions cool. One of the castle's original 33 wells was located in this

area. Today only 13 wells remain, the deepest with a 98 ft (30 m) drop.

The Tenshu rises 151 ft (46 m) above sea level. It sits atop Himeyama, a 69 ft (21 m) hill surrounded by an open plain. Himeji Castle is famous for its sophisticated defensive layout, which leads visitors on a convoluted

LEGENDS OF HIMEJI CASTLE

Himeji Castle is full of stories of intrigue, betrayal and sacrifice. Here are the stories of Okiku, Senhime and Sakura Genbei.

WHISPERS FROM OKIKU'S WELL

In 1470, Aoyama Tessan, a chief retainer of Kodera Norimoto, began plotting against his lord. Another of Kodera's retainers, Kinugasa Motonobu, grew suspicious and sent his girlfriend Kiku to spy on Aoyama. The plot was foiled. Aoyama was furious and falsely charged her with losing one of ten valuable dishes from the Aoyama's family treasure. She was tortured and her body thrown into a well. From then on, every night her sad voice could be heard counting dishes. Some believed there was a secret passageway at the bottom of the well leading out of the castle and the story had been concocted to prevent people going near the well. No passage, however, has ever been found.

THE MASTER CARPENTER'S DISTRESS

Sakura Genbei was the master carpenter of Himeji Castle. After the main tower was completed, he brought his wife to the castle to show her his work. Unfortunately, she observed that the tower seemed to be leaning slightly to the southeast. So distressed was Sakura by his poor workmanship that he climbed to the top of the tower and leapt to his death with a chisel in his mouth.

SENHIME

Princess Sen (Senhime) was the grand-daughter of Tokugawa Ieyasu. In a political alliance between the Tokugawa and Toyotomi houses in 1600, she was married to Toyotomi Hideyori (Toyotomi Hideyo-shi's son) when she was six years old. After Osaka Castle fell to an attack by her grandfather, Ieyasu, in 1615, Hideyori

committed ritual suicide (*seppuku*). Ieyasu promised Senhime's hand in marriage to whoever saved her from the burning castle. She was rescued but refused to marry her saviour because she had fallen in love with Honda Tadatoki, a handsome young samurai whom she met shortly after. Her heartbroken rescuer committed suicide. Senhime then married Honda and moved to Himeji Castle where they had a son, Kochiyo, and a daughter, Katsuhime. Her son died when he was three years old, and not long after her husband died of tuberculosis at the age of 31. In her grief, she became a Buddhist nun and returned to Edo where her brother Iemitsu, the third shogun, presented her with a beautiful mansion. She lived there until she was 70. Her daughter Katsu married Ikeda Mitsumasa, the Lord of Okayama, in Bizen province.

Opposite The Ninomon is a two-story tunnel gate (*anamon*). This gate slowed the advance of an attacking army by limiting the number of soldiers who could pass through the narrow, dark tunnel. Defending soldiers in the tower above could pull up the floorboards and attack intruders passing through.

Above The Hyakkenyagura is a 984 ft (300 m)-long corridor made up of a series of small rooms. Following the curve of the hill, it overlooks the Nishinomaru (western enclosure) where Honda Tadatoki and his wife, Princess Senhime, lived in their palace called Chushomaru. Princess Senhime's many maids-in-waiting lived in the Hyakkenyagura. The end room (closest) was called the Kesshoyagura (cosmetic tower). Princess Senhime came here to rest in private.

Above right Inside the Hyakkenyagura.

Right Located on the north side of the Sannomaru, the Hishinomon (diamond gate) vets access to the Ninomaru. The two-story Yaguramon (tower gate) has ornate bell-shaped windows (*katomado*) with gold leaf decoration.

Color key on page 37

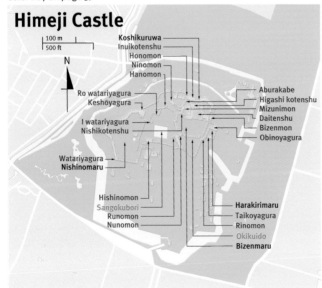

Himeji Castle

100 m
500 ft
N

Koshikuruwa
Inuikotenshu
Honomon
Ninomon
Hanomon
Ro watariyagura
Keshōyagura
I watariyagura
Nishikotenshu
Aburakabe
Higashi kotenshu
Mizunimon
Daitenshu
Bizenmon
Obinoyagura
Watariyagura
Nishinomaru
Hishinomon
Sangokubori
Runomon
Nunomon
Harakirimaru
Taikoyagura
Rinomon
Okikuido
Bizenmaru

Location Himeji, Hyogo prefecture
Nickname White Egret
Site area 54 acres (22 ha); original size 544 acres (220 ha)
Type Hirayamajiro
Layout Complex
Tenshu type Borogata, Renketsushiki (Compound)
Family crest Kuroda, Toyotomi, Ikeda, Honda, Sakai

Himeji

route to the inner enclosure. The castle is encircled by three spiraling moats, with an outer, medial and interior enclosure. Within the interior enclosure, the only one extant today, are Nishinomaru (western enclosure), Sannomaru (third enclosure) and Bizenmaru (innermost enclosure), a combined area of 54 acres (22 ha). The entire original castle occupied an area ten times that size. The living quarters of the Ikeda lords were located in the Bizenmaru, and for the Honda clan, the Sannomaru.

Of the 84 original gates, 21 remain at Himeji Castle. They take various forms, from highly decorated two-story tower gates, such as Hishino-mon, to a small opening in a stonewall (*uzumimon*). Other kinds of gates include ridgepole gates (*munemon*), Korean gates (*koraimon*) and tunnel gates (*anamon*). They are generally named according to the Japanese alphabet: I, Ro, Ha, Ni and so forth. The six gates near the main Tenshu are called Mizuichimon, Mizunimon (first water gate, second water gate,

etc.). Assigned tasters would check the water for poisoning each time they passed. Smaller gates close to the inner enclosure and Tenshu slowed down an invading army. Others could be blocked with stones.

ABURAKABE (OIL WALL)

It is believed that Toyotomi Hideyoshi built this wall in 1580. Composed of a mixture of mountain soil, pea gravel, rice washing water and rice porridge, the Aburakabe wall is as hard as concrete.

Above left As you approach the main Tenshu, the gates become narrower, lower and harder to break through. Visitors have to bend down to enter Mizuichimon, the first water gate, and Mizunimon (shown here), the second water gate. The small Rumon gate (**above**) could be filled in with rocks to block the enemy.

Left The Tenshu was used as a lookout, as a last line of defence and as a place to store weapons and provisions. Walls were lined with racks to hold guns, while gunpowder and fuses were hung in bags out of reach high up on the walls on bamboo hooks. When needed, a string was pulled, breaking the bamboo hook.

Eight different family crests can be seen on the end tiles at Himeji Castle, revealing the many changes in lords over the castle's history.

Cross

Kuroda Yoshitaka (Kanbei), 1567. Highly intelligent and a Christian, he was Toyotomi Hideyoshi's military advisor. He turned the castle over to Hideyoshi during the Western campaign of 1577–82.

Five-Three Paulownia Leaf

Toyotomi, 1580. Hashiba (Toyotomi) Hideyoshi built a three-story *tenshu* on Himeyama, which was completed in 1582. From here he launched the campaign against Tottori Castle and the water siege of Takamatsu Castle.

During the Tokugawa period (1603–1868), 31 lords were sent to Himeji Castle. The importance of this location as a gateway between the eastern and western provinces meant that if a lord was sickly or too young, the shogun replaced him immediately. Most of the *daimyo* who had been on the Toyotomi side at the Battle of Sekigahara in 1600, and were thus outside lords, lived in the western provinces, so were never trusted by the Tokugawa shogunate and had to be closely watched.

Butterfly With Raised Wings

Ikeda, 1600. After the Battle of Sekigahara in 1600, Tokugawa Ieyasu placed Ikeda Terumasa at Himeji Castle with an income of 980,000 *koku*. Although Ikeda had initially been antagonistic toward Tokugawa Ieyasu, being allied to Oda Nobunaga and Toyotomi Hideyoshi, he married Ieyasu's second daughter on the orders of Toyotomi Hideyoshi to cement political and military alliances. He was popularly known as the commander of western Japan. Ikeda rebuilt and enlarged the castle from 1601 to 1609 using the latest technology and assisted by the western *daimyo*, as required by the shogun. After 18 years, however, his heir, Mitsumasa, was transferred to Tottori.

Standing Hollyhock Trefoil

Honda Tadamasa, 1617. He was a principle

supporter of the Tokugawa family and the son of Takakatsu, who was a great friend of Tokugawa Ieyasu. Honda was appointed to command the western region of Japan. He undertook extensive civil engineering projects, adding the third enclosure (Sannomaru) and western enclosure (Nishinomaru), expanding the castle itself and dredging the Senba River to connect the castle to nearby Shikama by boat. His son Tadatoki married Senhime (Princess Sen),

Tokugawa Ieyasu's granddaughter, who had been married to Toyotomi Hideyori when she was six.

Water Plantain

Matsudaira Tadaaki, 1639. The adopted

heir by his grandfather Tokugawa Ieyasu, he died at the castle after only five years. His heir, Tadahiro, was found to be an underachiever and consequently was transferred to Yamagata in northeast Japan.

Three Tomoe, Whorls

Matsudaira Naomoto, 1648. Grandson of

Ieyasu and fourth son of the second shogun, Hidetada, he was transferred from Yamagata to Edo Castle but fell ill and died before assuming his post at Himeji Castle.

Genji Wheel

Sakakibara Tadatsugu, 1649. He carried out extensive repairs on the castle in 1657.

Spear Points Around Wood Sorrell

Sakai Tadazumi, 1747. The Sakai family remained at Himeji for 120 years.

SUBSTITUTE STONES

Building stones were scarce when Toyotomi Hideyoshi built the original three-story Tenshu at Himeji in 1580. Many were donated or appropriated, such as lantern bases from temples, stone coffins and even the millstone from an old local woman. A lantern base can be seen at the Hamon. A millstone is visible near the entrance to the Koshikuruwa and a stone coffin now sits at the Bizenmon.

DIRECTIONS

The castle is a 15 minute walk from the north exit of JR Himeji Station or a 5 minute bus ride.

Hikone Castle 1602–1622

Hikone Castle was established on the route between Edo and Kyoto in order to monitor the Toyotomi family in Osaka and their supporters in the west of Japan. Omi province had been the domain of Ishida Mitsunari, who led the Toyotomi loyalists at the Battle of Sekigahara in 1600 against the Tokugawa. After Ishida's defeat, his castle at Sawayama was destroyed and the province awarded to one of Tokugawa Ieyasu's most trusted and influential generals, Ii Naomasa.

Ii Naomasa led the Red Devils, a corps of fierce warriors who wore red lacquered armor and carried red banners into battle.

Ii died of battle wounds in 1601 before he could begin construction of a castle on the nearby site of Hikone. His son Naokatsu began the project in 1602, assisted by the Minister of Construction and 12 lords on orders from the Tokugawa shogunate. Taking 20 years to complete, the castle offered excellent defensive and offensive capabilities but, fortunately, was never

Right Along with keeping intruders out, gates proclaimed the importance of the lord. Unsightly nail heads were covered with nail coverings (*kugi-kakushi*) in the shape of flowers, spears, circles or diamonds. Behind this door to the Tenbinyagura tower, the dry stonewall reveals how the wall was constructed. Chisels mark on the large stones show the method used to split stones. Gaps between the large stones were filled with small pebbles that could be removed and used as missiles in the event of an invasion.

Far right The Nishinomarusanjuyagura, the three-story tower in the western enclosure, protected the western side of the castle. The path leads to the Kuromon.

Left The small but beautifully proportioned Tenshu is over 400 years old. Cusped gables, bell-shaped windows and the contrasting colors of white plaster, black timber and gold leaf make this one of the most stunning original Tenshu in Japan today.

Above The Tenbinyagura (balancing scale tower) at Hikone Castle protected the southeast side of the castle. To approach the castle, it is necessary to turn 180 degrees under the wooden bridge, then make another 180 degree turn to approach the Tenbinyagura. Castle defenders could fire down on intruders from their elevated positions overlooking the approach. The wooden bridge could also be demolished, cutting off access to the inner enclosure. The stone base on the right-hand side of the Tenbinyagura is in the *gobozumi* style of piling. The left was reconstructed in the Edo era and is in the *uchikomihagi* style. The Tenbinyagura was originally the Otemon (main gate) of Toyotomi Hideyoshi's Nagahama Castle and was transferred here around 1603. It is the only example of a gate of this shape in Japan.

attacked. Before long, Naomasa's son Naokatsu proved himself to be incompetent and was replaced by his illegitimate brother, Naotaka. Naotaka successfully led the Ii contingent into battle at the siege of Osaka Castle in 1614. As a result, he inherited Hikone Castle and its surrounding province with an annual income of 350,000 *koku*. Fourteen lords from the Ii clan subsequently ruled Hikone for the next 260 years. The head of the Ii clan held the important post of Tairo, great councillor to the Tokugawa shogun, throughout the Edo era.

POINTS OF INTEREST

Hikone Castle has a number of original buildings within its extensive grounds, many of which are unique among Japanese castles today: the Umaya (horse stables), the Tenbin-yagura (balancing gate), the adjacent Genkyuen garden with residences and a tea house, and the Umoreginoya (lodge). Ii Naosuke, the 13th lord of the Hikone clan, studied martial arts, poetry and tea ceremony at the lodge before entering the government at Edo.

The three-level Tenshu in the Honmaru combines skilfully gabled roofs (*kirizumahafu*), half-hipped roofs (*irimoyahafu*) and cusped gables (*karahafu*). Black cusped windows (*katomado*) and push out windows (*renjimado*) contrast dramatically with the white plastered walls, gold decoration and gray roof tiles. The Tenshu, originally constructed at Otsu in 1575, was moved to Hikone in 1602. It is an older *borogata* style of keep housing a watchtower on the top floor. Instead of a huge central pillar (*toshibashira*) running from the basement to the top of the structure, which is usual in multilevel Japanese buildings, each successive floor of the Tenshu was an independent addition.

Four hidden rooms (*kakushibeya*) are found within the Tenshu under the projecting roof gables on the east and west side of the second floor, and on the north and south side of the third floor. Each room is large enough to fit five people. Hidden shooting holes (*tepposama*) line the walls of the Tenshu. Plastered over on the outside, they could be easily pierced in the event of an attack. Inside they appear as wooden apertures, either square or triangular in shape. The north side of the Tenshu has a double wall filled with stones, making it bulletproof. Entry to the Tenshu is through the adjoining single-story Tamonyagura.

The grounds of Hikone are extensive, covering around 62 acres (25 ha).

Above The Jihosho (time-keeping bell) was originally located in the lower Kanenomaru. It was moved higher up to the entrance to the Honmaru by the 12th lord, Ii Naoaki, in order that its sound would reach the entire castle town. It is still rung five times a day.

Above right A view of the lake in the Genkyuen from the Hoshodai (guest house). The Ii lords of Hikone entertained their most distinguished guests here.

Right The Rakuraken is built in the *goten* (palace) style. It is a one-story building with large sliding screens which can be opened or removed to enjoy the surrounding gardens.

Opposite top left The apex of the roof of the Umaya (stable). A dozen horses belonging to successive lords of the Hikone clan were kept here. An Important Cultural Asset, it is the only extant stable within castles grounds in Japan.

Opposite top center The plastered apex of the Ninomaru-sawaguchi-tamonyagura, which protects the entrance to the Nishinomaru. Plastering the timber buildings afforded greater protection against fire.

Opposite top right The original timber beams inside the 400-year-old Tenshu.

Below Situated at the foot of the inner castle grounds, the Genkyuen garden was constructed in 1677. Landscaped around a large pond, the garden is believed to be modeled on the detached palace of Emperor Genso of the Tang dynasty in ancient China. Trees and rocks imitating the Eight Views of the Omi region, Chikubu Island and the White Rocks of Oki are artfully arranged in the garden. Successive generations of Ii Lords entertained guests in the Hoshodai beside the lake.

Moats surround the entire site, with enclosures separated by the middle and inner moats. The original garden and other extant buildings outside the outer moat provide an idea of the castle complex as it existed in the seventeenth century.

DIRECTIONS

A 15 minute walk up the main road northwest of Hikone Station. Five minutes by taxi.

Color key on page 37

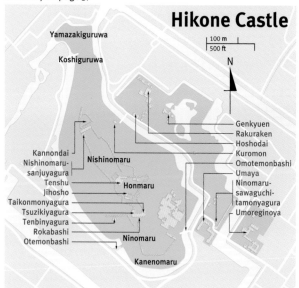

Hikone Castle

Yamazakiguruwa	
Koshiguruwa	

100 m
500 ft

N

Genkyuen
Rakuraken
Hoshodai
Kuromon
Omotemonbashi
Umaya
Ninomaru-sawaguchi-tamonyagura
Umoreginoya

Kannondai
Nishinomaru-sanjuyagura · Nishinomaru
Tenshu
Jihosho · Honmaru
Taikonmonyagura
Tsuzikiyagura
Tenbinyagura
Rokabashi
Otemonbashi · Ninomaru

Kanenomaru

Location Hikone, Shiga prefecture
Nickname Kingame
Site area 62 acres (25 ha), perimeter 2.5 miles (4 km)
Type Hirayamajiro
Layout Renkaku
Tenshu type Borogata, Fukugoshiki (Attached)
Family crest Ii

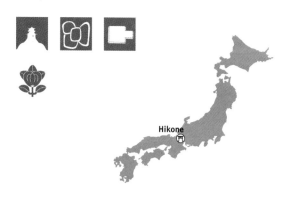

Nijo Castle 1602

Nijo Castle was built by Tokugawa Ieyasu in 1602. After his victory at the Battle of Sekigahara in 1600, Ieyasu needed to send a clear message to the emperor and warlords throughout Japan that the Tokugawa had taken over from the Toyotomi as the most powerful *daimyo*. All western *daimyo* were ordered to assist in construction as retribution for opposing the Tokugawa at the Battle of Sekigahara. This strategy depleted their resources, thereby limiting their ability to rebel against the new Tokugawa shogunate. On completion of the sumptuous Ninomaru Palace in 1603, Ieyasu entertained royal courtiers and feudal lords over three days in celebration of his installation as shogun. Nijo Castle was subsequently used as a base for the shoshidai, the Tokugawa shogunate's governor of Kyoto, whose main role was to monitor the activities of the emperor and his court.

Several significant events took place at Nijo Castle during the Tokugawa reign from 1603 to 1868. In 1611, 18-year-old Toyotomi Hideyori, accompanied by Kato Kiyomasa from Kumamoto, was fatefully interviewed by Tokugawa Ieyasu. Unfortunately, Hideyori's intellect and competences were considered a potential threat to the stability of the new Tokugawa shogunate. Ieyasu thus set out to destroy Hideyori and the Toyotomi line. This he did by besieging Osaka Castle in 1614 and 1615, using Nijo Castle as his headquarters. Hideyori's ally, Kato Kiyomasa, meanwhile, had died suddenly of suspected poisoning upon his return from Nijo Castle.

Left Over 400 years old, the Ninomarugoten (1603–26) is a rare extant example of a *shoin*-style palace of the early Edo era. Comprising a series of five linked buildings—Tozamurai, Shikidai, Ohiroma, Kuroshoin and Shiroshoin—the palace presides over a pond and rock garden. The precious interior paintings are by artists of the famous Edo era Kano School.

Below The Ninomarugoten Karamon was taken from Fushimi Castle in the early seventeenth century. Its elaborate decoration is typical of the style of the Azuchi-Momoyama era (1576–1600). During renovations in 2013, workers discovered a metal Imperial chrysanthemum emblem covering an earlier hollyhock crest of the Tokugawa, indicating an attempt to erase traces of former ownership.

In 1626, Nijo Castle was renovated and its grounds extended. The innermost enclosure, Honmaru, was added, more residential buildings were erected and the five-story Tenshu from Fushimi Castle was relocated to the southwest corner of the Honmaru. These renovations were undertaken in preparation for a visit from Emperor Gomizuno-o, who stayed for five days and was lavishly entertained by the retired Shogun Hidetada and his son, the third shogun, Iemitsu. Once again, this intense building program and elaborate festivities served to display the might of the Tokugawa shogunate.

In 1634, Shogun Tokugawa Iemitsu led a force of 300,000 men to Kyoto in a show of military might to the Imperial court and the *daimyo* of western Japan. This was the last visit of any shogun to the Imperial court until the Meiji Restoration. In 1750, the castle's Tenshu was struck by lightning and destroyed. A new tower was deemed unnecessary and so the Tenshu remained in ruins. The Honmaru palaces were destroyed in Kyoto's Great Fire of 1788.

In 1867, in response to the Imperial court and several southern *daimyo*, the 15th-generation Shogun Tokugawa Yoshinobu assembled all feudal lords in Nijo Castle's Ohiroma to witness his declaration of the restoration of Imperial rule. The following year, Emperor Meiji visited Nijo Castle where he ordered the subjugation of the *bakufu* (shogunal government) at an assembly held in the Shiroshoin. The Tokugawa family were declared criminals. Nijo Castle was therefore the site of the beginning and the end of the Tokugawa reign.

The Imperial court requisitioned the buildings and grounds in 1872. Jurisdiction over the castle was transferred to the Kyoto Prefectural

Opposite below The front gate of Nijo Castle, called Higashiotemon, is a two-story gatehouse set into a stonewall. The enormous timber gate is reinforced with iron. To the left is the Bansho (guardhouse) built in 1608. Some 50 guards were stationed here at a time between the years 1634 and 1863.

Below Superb craftsmanship and attention to detail at Nijo Castle reveal the Tokugawa's intention to impress as much as to create a stronghold.

Left The former Katsuranomiya Palace, built in 1847, was removed from its original site and rebuilt in the Honmaru in 1893. The original palace on this site came from Fushimi Castle in 1626 but was destroyed by fire in 1788.

Below left The white plastered mud wall originally extended from the corner towers around the perimeter of the castle grounds. Stone-dropping windows and shooting holes were located at strategic points.

Below right View of the Uchibori (inner moat) and Nishibashi (west bridge) from the 49 ft (15 m)-high Tenshu base in the Honmaru. The five-story Tenshu was relocated from Fushimi Castle in 1626. It was never rebuilt after being struck by lightning in 1750 and destroyed.

Office. In 1885, the site was renamed the Nijo Detached Palace, with responsibility for the site passing to the Imperial Household Department. The old palace of the Katsura Imperial family was relocated from the Kyoto Imperial Palace to the Honmaru where it can be seen today. In 1939, the site was donated to Kyoto City, and in 1994 UNESCO registered it as a World Cultural Heritage Site.

POINTS OF INTEREST

There are numerous Important Cultural Properties within the 69 acre (28 ha) Nijo Castle site: the Ninomaru-goten karamon (gate to the second enclosure), Tsujibei (long earthern wall), Daidokoro (kitchen), Higashi-otemon (eastern front gate), Nino-

Below The Ninomaru garden is conceived around a large pond bordered by various sized stones. In the pond's center are three islands: Horaijima (Island of Eternal Happiness), Tsurujima (Crane Island), and Kamejima (Turtle Island). The design of the garden is attributed to the famous tea master and landscape designer Kobori Enshu. The Kuroshoin of the Ninomarugoten is on the right.

Left Timber supports in the plastered mud wall that surrounds Nijo Castle.

Right The ornate decoration in the ceiling of the Karamon is typical of the ostentatious Momoyama period, named after Toyotomi Hideyoshi's Fushimi Castle at Momoyama.

maru tonan sumiyagura (southeast corner turret), Ninomaru seinan sumiyagura (southwest corner turret) Ninomarudozo (storehouse), Honmarugoten (inner enclosure palace) and Ninomaru kita otemon (north gate).

The Ninomarugoten is an important surviving example of the lavish Azuchi-Momoyama style. The palace consists of five linked buildings, staggered to afford a view over the Ninomaru garden and central pond, designed by the famous tea master and landscape designer Kobori Enshu

(1579–1647). Constructed of cypress (*hinoki*), the palace comprises 33 rooms and covers an area of 800 *tatami* mats. The interior holds many precious examples of fine art from the Azuchi-Momoyama era. Sliding doors and walls are covered in gold leaf and depictions of tigers, leopards, bamboo, pine trees, herons and flora have been painted by artists of the Kano School. Ornate transoms carved out of massive cypress blocks hang above the sliding doors.

The wooden floors from the entrance of the Ninomarugoten to

the Ohiroma (grand chambers) 'squeak' when walked on. The bird-like sound of the Uguisubari ('Nightingale floor') provides a warning to the occupants of intruders entering the complex.

DIRECTIONS
Bus No. 9, 50 or 101 from JR Kyoto Station to Nijo jo mae bus stop (15 minutes).

Subway Tozai Line to Nijo jo mae Station (10 minutes).

Color key on page 37

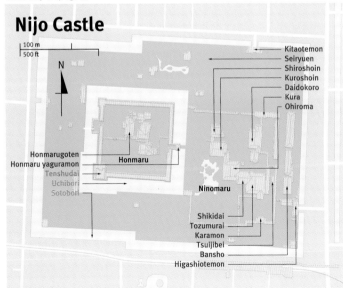

Nijo Castle

100 m / 500 ft

Kitaotemon
Seiryuen
Shiroshoin
Kuroshoin
Daidokoro
Kura
Ohiroma

Honmarugoten
Honmaru yaguramon
Tenshudai
Uchibori
Sotobori

Honmaru

Ninomaru

Shikidai
Tozumurai
Karamon
Tsuijibei
Bansho
Higashiotemon

Location Kyoto, Kyoto prefecture
Site area 69 acres (28 ha)
Type Hirajiro
Layout Doshinen
Tenshu type Dokuritsushiki (independant)
Family crest Tokugawa

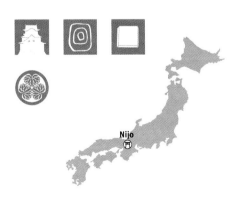

Nijo

Osaka Castle 1583

Opposite above The eight-story Tenshu of Osaka Castle is located in the Honmaru.

Opposite below Huge stones flank the Oteguchi (main entrance) as a way to impress visitors to the castle.

The location of Osaka Castle has made it one of the most contested sites in Japanese history. Meaning 'great slope,' the raised ground of Osaka is surrounded by rivers to the north and east and by the sea to the west, making it difficult to siege yet easy to defend. Located in central Japan, Osaka was close to the Imperial capital of Kyoto and accessible to both the western and northern provinces.

Osaka was initially the site of the Ishiyama Honganji, a temple belonging to the Jodo Shinsho (Pure Land) Buddhist sect. These powerful militant monks stood in the way of Oda Nobunaga's quest to unify Japan in the mid-sixteenth century. After years of unsuccessfully trying to eject them, an agreement was reached in 1580 with the aid of the Imperial court. Ikeda Shonyu, one of Nobunaga's vassals, then occupied the site.

Toyotomi Hideyoshi became Japan's most powerful warlord following Nobunaga's death in 1582. He chose Osaka as the site to build his castle. Using the resources of the *daimyo* now under his control, Toyotomi built a castle to rival Oda's revolutionary Azuchi Castle in scale, strength and opulence. Construction began in 1583, with the work lasting five years. Approximately 100,000 laborers drawn from every province worked day and night on the castle. Some 60,000 men toiled for three months to dig the inner and outer moats, about 1.8 miles (3 km) and 5 miles (8 km) in length, respectively, and up to 23 ft (7 m) deep and 295 ft (90 m) wide. Timber for the enormous project was hauled from 28 provinces.

Left Osaka Castle's fan-shaped stonewalls rise more than 65.6 ft (20 m) above the moats. The castle grounds are laid out in the *doshinen* style, wherby the Honmaru (inner enclosure) is surrounded by an inner moat, with an outer moat surrounding the outer enclosures. The main entrance to the castle (at left) leads to a *masugatamon* (box-shaped gate). A small *koraimon* (post-and-beam gate) allows access to a large courtyard, surrounded on two sides with a long tower from which soldiers were stationed. Upon entering the *koraimon*, it was necessary to turn left to go through the *yaguramon* (tower gate) to gain access to the Nishinomaru (western enclosure).

Toyotomi Hideyoshi died in 1598, leaving his five-year-old heir, Hideyori, in the care of five regents. One of these men, Maeda Toshiie, moved to Osaka as Hideyori's guardian and the governor of the castle. However, when Maeda died the following year, the remaining four

regents proved unable to govern together, resulting in a showdown at Sekigahara in 1600. This battle between *daimyo* loyal to Toyotomi Hideyoshi (the western or 'loyalist' forces) and the eastern army led by Tokugawa Ieyasu, was won by the Tokugawa side, giving Tokugawa

Above The Senganyagura protected the Oteguchi (main entrance) of the castle. Built in 1620, this two-story tower is one of the oldest buildings at Osaka Castle. The Nishisotobori (west outer moat) is in the foreground.

Below The Inuiyagura (northwest tower) is the oldest tower at Osaka Castle. It is unusual as the first and second stories are of equal size. The stone-dropping windows hang over the stonewall to enable defenders to drop missiles onto attackers scaling the wall below. Window shutters were covered in plaster to minimize flammability in the event of an attack.

Tokugawa shogunate remained whilst Hideyori was alive. On the pretext of being insulted by the wording on a bell Hideyori had cast in 1614, Ieyasu laid siege to Osaka Castle in the winter of 1614–15. Many of the outer moats were filled in and defenses destroyed. The Tokugawa forces returned in the following summer of 1615. This time Osaka Castle was razed and Hideyori and his mother, Yodogimi, committed ritual suicide.

Osaka Castle was now in the hands of the Tokugawa shogunate. In recognition of its strategic importance, Ieyasu's son, Shogun Tokugawa Hidetada, began reconstruction in 1620. Sixty-four *tozama* (outside lords) from western and northern Japan were called upon to assist in the building between 1620 and 1629. Osaka Castle remained in Tokugawa hands until the Meiji Restoration. Under the Meiji government, the castle became part of the Osaka Army Arsenal, manufacturing guns, ammunition and explosives for the Japanese army. During World War II, it was one of the Imperial Japanese Army's largest armories.

POINTS OF INTEREST

The vast grounds, majestic fan-shaped stonewalls and extensive moats all herald the importance of Osaka Castle. Enclosures are laid out as concentric rings delineated by wet and dry moats. The wet outer moat is divided by four ramps providing access to the inner enclosures. Each ramp has a fortified gatehouse on the inner side. Dry moats were excavated near important gates, such as the Sakuramon, to prevent enemy boats

absolute control over the *daimyo*. Hideyori remained at Osaka Castle and Ieyasu gave him the provinces of Settsu, Kawachi and Izumi with an annual revenue totaling 650,000 *koku*. To further display his allegiance to Hideyori, the newly appointed Shogun Tokugawa Ieyasu promised the hand of his six-year-old granddaughter in marriage.

Although the Tokugawa shogunate spent the next 12 years consolidating their power by reshuffling *daimyo* territories, issuing strict laws for military houses and depleting their enemies' resources through building campaigns, the threat of Toyotomi loyalists raising an army against the

Above This style of semicircular plaster and stone shooting hole is rarely seen at other castles.

Left The corner of the Tenshu base is precisely cut in the *sangizumi* (zipper) style. Stone-dropping windows protect the vulnerable corners of the base, the easiest part of the walls to scale.

Below A stone and timber shooting hole. The semicircle at the top and the funnel-shaped stone opening enabled soldiers to take aim at invaders.

Color key on page 37

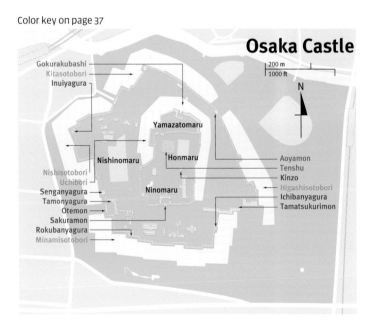

Osaka Castle

200 m
1000 ft

N

Gokurakubashi
Kitasotobori
Inuiyagura

Yamazatomaru

Honmaru

Nishinomaru

Aoyamon
Tenshu
Kinzo
Higashisotobori
Ichibanyagura
Tamatsukurimon

Nishisotobori
Uchibori
Senganyagura
Tamonyagura
Otemon
Sakuramon
Rokubanyagura
Minamisotobori

Ninomaru

Location Osaka, Osaka prefecture
Nickname Kin Castle
Site area 15 acres (6 ha)
Type Hirajiro
Layout Doshinen
Tenshu type Borogata,Dokuritsushiki (Independent)
Family crest Toyotomi, Tokugawa

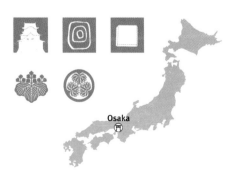

Osaka

Left A view of the Inuiyagura (northwest tower), Osaka Castle's oldest tower. The corner of its fan-shaped stone base is precisely cut in the *sangizumi* (zipper) style.

Right The reconstructed Tenshu at Osaka Castle has eight stories, is in the independent style and has a watchtower on its uppermost story. The design of this 1931 concrete reconstruction was taken from historic screen paintings of Toyotomi Hide-yoshi's original black keep.

from drawing close during an attack. The nearby rivers were used to fill the wet moats. This layout is uncommon since extensive earthworks were needed to create the ring of moats. However, since the castle belonged to the supreme military leader, an abundant workforce was readily available. Both Toyotomi Hideyoshi and Tokugawa Hidetada exploited the resources of *daimyo* under their control in 1583 and 1620, respectively. Contributions by these *daimyo* are marked by family crest inscriptions on the stonewalls, many of which can

be seen in the Kakushikuruwa in the Yamazatomaru. Some *daimyo* contributed enormous stones, which were emplaced at important entrances. The largest stone at Osaka Castle, measuring 640 sq ft (60 sq m), is situated directly through the Sakura-mon, the gateway into the Honmaru. Called the Takoishi (octopus stone), it was positioned here by Okayama *daimyo* Ikeda Tadao. Ikeda was also responsible for the huge stones positioned at the Kyobashiguchi (entrance): the Higoishi, with a surface area of 580 sq ft (54 sq m),

and the Kyobashiguchi-nibanishi, with an area of 387 sq ft (36 sq m).

The current Tenshu is a 1931 concrete replica of Toyotomi Hideyo-shi's original keep, burnt down in the Siege of Osaka in 1615. Its design was copied from screen paintings. These historic depictions, however, show the Tenshu as black, whereas the reconstruction is white. The current Tenshu has eight floors and houses a museum on the history of Osaka Castle. It sits atop an impressive base of perfectly cut and aligned rocks in the *kirikomi-hagi* style of stone piling. Tokugawa

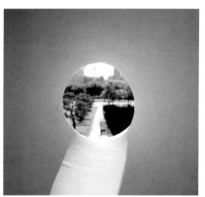

Hidetada's Tenshu was a different design and was located elsewhere in the Honmaru. This keep was destroyed in 1868 by Tokugawa troops retreating from Imperial forces.

Thirteen structures at Osaka Castle are designated Important Cultural Assets: Ichibanyagura and Rokuban-yagura (1628), the Kinzo storehouse (1751), Inuiyagura on the west outer moat and Senganyagura (1620), the Otemon, Sakuramon, Tamonyagura, Kinmeisui well and a number of sections of the castle walls around the front gate (Otemon).

Opposite below far left A round plastered shooting hole looks down the approach to the Otemon.

Opposite below center The Kakushikuruwa was an area in the castle where soldiers could hide from enemies. This enclosure had only one narrow exit, making it difficult to see. Many crests of *daimyo* charged with building the castle are inscribed on stones in the walls here.

Opposite below right The most common type of dry stonewall, *uchikomihagi* (rough cut piling).

DIRECTIONS

There are numerous ways to get to Osaka Castle: via the subway, getting off at either Temmabashi Station, Tanimachi Station, Morinomiya Station or Osaka Business Park Station; via the JR train line, getting off at Morinomiya Station, Osakajo koen Station or Osakajo Kitazume Station; via the city bus, getting off at Otemae; via Keihan, Temmabashi Station and the Aqualiner, getting off at Osakajo harbor. Entry to Osaka Castle park is free, with a charge to enter the museum.

Kanazawa Castle 1583–1599

K anazawa Castle was the seat of the powerful Maeda family from 1583 until the Meiji Restoration in 1868. With an annual income of nearly 1,200,000 *koku*, the Maeda were the wealthiest *daimyo* after the Tokugawa shogun. Their influence spread with separate family branches installed at Toyama and Daishoji.

Kanazawa Castle is protected by rivers to the east and west, the Sea of Japan to the north and the Hakusan mountains to the south. The elevated site was first occupied in 1546 by militant Buddhists of the Kyoto Honganji sect. Their teachings of Ikko-shu, the 'single-minded religion,' appealed to many local farmers who joined the faith. Oda Nobunaga's

army defeated these militant Buddhist monks in 1580 after which his vassal, Sakuma Morimasa, erected a castle on the site. Following Oda's death in 1582, Toyotomi Hideyoshi assumed control of Japan and gave Kanazawa city and part of Ishikawa to his friend Maeda Toshiie in reward for loyal service. Maeda entered the city of Kanazawa in 1583.

Maeda Toshiie was a fierce warrior known as Yari no Mataza (Mataza the Spearman). He worked his way up from being Oda Nobunaga's pageboy at 13, with an income of 125 *koku*, to become one of the wealthiest and most powerful *daimyo*, with an annual income of nearly 1,000,000 *koku* by 1599. Although a loyal friend and ally

of Toyotomi Hideyoshi, he was careful not to take sides and established an alliance with Tokugawa Ieyasu by engaging his three-year-old son, Toshitsune, to Ieyasu's five-year-old granddaughter in 1595. During the next six generations, both families continued to intermarry, with the twelfth, thirteenth and fourteenth Tokugawa shoguns descendants of the Maeda clan.

Maeda Toshiie was one of the five regents charged with governing the country in the name of Toyotomi Hideyoshi's son, Hideyori, in 1598. However, Toshiie died the following year. After the Battle of Sekigahara in 1600, Toshiie's wife, Maeda Matsu, assured the safety of the Maeda clan

Left and below left Ishikawamon is one of three barbican-style gates at Kanazawa Castle. This heavily fortified gate is accessed through the central post-and-beam gate. The inner courtyard is surrounded by towers from which defenders could shoot. On the left is a two-story tower, directly ahead a one-story tower and on the right a two-story gatehouse with iron-plated doors.

Right Gojikkennagaya, Hashizumemon-tsuzukiyagura and Hishiyagura (in foreground), viewed from the Sannomaru (third enclosure). These buildings protected the Ninomaru palace and administrative buildings. The Hishiyagura (diamond tower) is a 56 ft (17 m)-high three-story building on a 38 ft (11.7 m) stone base. Its name derived from its diamond-shaped walls, with angles of 80 and 100 degrees. The posts are also diamond shaped, requiring sophisticated construction techniques during the 2001 reconstruction. The Hishiyagura was used as a watchtower and place where the lord met his vassals. The Gojikken-nagaya was a store for weapons. The Hashizumemon-tsuzukiyagura guarded the gateway between the Sannomaru and Ninomaru.

by voluntarily going to Edo as a hostage of the Tokugawa. Toshiie's heir, Toshinaga, cleverly sided with Tokugawa Ieyasu against Uesugi Kagekatsu in the months leading up to the battle. For this he was given the fief taken from his brother Toshimasa who had fought with the losing Toyotomi loyalists. Toshinaga became the wealthiest *daimyo* after Ieyasu, with an annual income of 1,195,000 *koku*. He retired to Toyama Castle in 1605 and was succeeded by another brother, Toshitsune.

Numerous fires destroyed Kanazawa Castle. The Tenshu built by the first lord, Maeda Toshiie, in the Honmaru (main enclosure) was struck by lightning and burnt down in 1602. This was never rebuilt and the functions of the feudal government were moved to the lower second enclosure, Ninomaru. The surviving

palace in the Honmaru then burnt down in 1620. It was reconstructed the following year but burnt down again ten years later, in 1631. A new palace was constructed in the Ninomaru in 1632. Some 120 years later, in 1759, another fire nearly gutted the entire castle. The Ninomaru palace and Hashizumemon were reconstructed in 1762. In 1808, the Ninomaru palace was burnt down yet again along with the Hishiyagura. Both were reconstructed shortly after.

In 1869, the fourteenth Maeda lord returned his land and title to the government to be used as a military barracks. Fire razed the Ninomaru palace, Hashizumemon and Gojikken-nagaya in 1881. Occupied by Kanazawa University from 1949 to 1995, the site was purchased by the Ishikawa Prefectural Government and turned into a public park. The current

Above left A small *koraimon* allows entry from the Sannomaru into the heavily defended courtyard of the Hashizumemon.

Above right The Kahokumon is the front gate leading to the Sannomaru. Located on top of Kahoku zaka (Kahoku hill), it comprises the Ichinomon (first gate), Ninomon (second gate), *dobei* (earthern walls surrounding the courtyard) and Niramiyaguradai (watchtower). The timber shooting holes beside the Ichinomon are accessed by climbing the stone steps. The small opening is plastered on the exterior wall and broken whenever necessary.

Hashizumemon, Gojikkennagaya, Hishiyagura, Tsuzukiyagura and Kahokumon have all been reconstructed using authentic materials and traditional construction techniques.

POINTS OF INTEREST

Kanazawa Castle comprises 12 enclosures. Four major moats encircle the site with two smaller moats dividing the inner enclosures. The

Left The complex layout created by gates, towers, enclosures and mud walls deterred would-be attackers and slowed down intruders who penetrated the castle grounds.

Right Sea cucumber walls (*namakobei*) are a feature of Kanazawa Castle. The stone tiles add an extra layer of protection to the plastered mud walls. The rounded raised plaster between the tiles gives these walls the name of the sea cucumber (*namako*). The small tower has a trapdoor overhanging the moat. This can be lifted from inside the tower and stones or other such missiles thrown down onto intruders.

CASTLES OF THE MAEDA FAMILY

Arako

Maeda Toshiharu was lord of Arako in Owari (Aichi prefecture). He was paid 5,000 *koku* to fight for Oda Nobunaga. His fourth son, Toshiie, born in 1538, became a page for Oda Nobunaga when he was 13. An aggressive fighter, Toshiie was rewarded after each battle with additional revenue. By 1568 his income had grown to around 1,000 *koku*. In 1579. Toshiie was nominated by Nobunaga as lord of Arako, replacing his father.

Nanao

Oda Nobunaga gave Maeda Toshiie the Noto area in 1581, where he built Nanao Castle. He received an annual income of 200,000 *koku*. The remains of field stone walls can be seen at the site.

Kanazawa

In 1583, Toshiie was granted Kanazawa city and part of Ishikawa for his loyal service to Toyotomi Hideyoshi.

Komatsu

On his way home from defeating the lord of Daishyoji Castle in 1600, Toshiie's son, Maeda Toshinaga, fought Niwa Nagashige, lord of Komatsu Castle. Niwa was later removed from his post and Komatsu Castle became part of the Maeda holdings. A new castle was built at Komatsu in 1640 for Maeda Toshitsune, the third lord of Kanazawa Castle, to retire to. Originally constructed in a weedy swamp surrounded by the Kakehashi River, it was also called the 'Floating Castle.' Inmates from Komatsu prison, acting on government orders, destroyed it in 1872. Only the stone base remains.

Toyama

Toyama Castle was originally built in 1543 by a powerful clan led by Mizukoshi Katsuhige. In 1581, the governor of Toyama, Sassa Narimasa (appointed by Oda Nobunaga), strengthened and improved the castle defences. After Oda Nobunaga's death, Narimasa was unsuccessful in his campaign to defeat Oda's successor, Toyotomi Hideyoshi. Toyama Castle and the surrounding areas were given to Toshinaga Maeda in 1585. His eldest son, Toshimasa, took charge of the castle in 1597. It burnt down in 1609 and lay neglected until 1639 when Toshitsugu, the second son of Toshitsune, moved in. Thirteen generations of Maeda ruled Toyama over a period of 232 years until the Meiji Restoration. The Tenshu was destroyed in air raids during World War II. The current Tenshu is a concrete reconstruction.

Takaoka

A new castle was built at Takaoka after Toyama Castle burnt down in 1609. No castle buildings remain, although the grounds have been turned into a park surrounded by the original moats.

Daishoji

Maeda Toshitsune split Kaga han into three provinces in 1639, creating Daishoji han in Enuma gun, and Toyama han in Etchu ken. He installed his second son, Toshitsugi, as the first lord of Toyama and his third son, Toshiharu, as the first lord of Daishoji, the castle of Yamaguchi Munenaga, who was defeated by Maeda Toshinaga in 1600.

Above Kahokumon taken from the Sannomaru looking back into the courtyard of the gate. Soldiers could fire down onto intruders from this two-story *yaguramon* (two-story gatehouse).

Above The Gojikkennagaya and Hashizumemon from the Ninomaru.

Honmaru, situated on the highest ground, originally contained three towers and the lord's residence. Next in importance was the Ninomaru where the lord's palace was built after fire destroyed the Honmaru in 1631. The Sannomaru and the Tsurunomaru had to be crossed before reaching the Ninomaru and Honmaru. Two *masugatamon* (barbican-style gateways) protected the Ninomaru, Ishikawamon and Kahokumon.

The timber stone-dropping windows with an undulating gable (*karahafu*) are unique to Kanazawa Castle.

Sea cucumber walls (*namakobei*), so-named because the raised plaster between the tiles resembles the shape of a sea cucumber (*namako*), are a feature of Kanazawa Castle. The stone tiles attached to a plastered wall provide strength and protect the plaster from the elements.

Kanazawa Castle lies beside Kenrokuen, one of Japan's most celebrated gardens. The fifth lord, Tsunanori, started the gardens, which were expanded by the twelfth and thirteenth lords. Three sets of contrasting garden elements were created: spaciousness and seclusion, artifice and antiquity, and watercourses and panoramas, giving rise to the name *ken* (combined), *roku* (six), *en* (garden).

DIRECTIONS

10 minutes by taxi or bus from Kanazawa Station. 20 minutes walk from the station.

Color key on page 37

Kanazawa Castle

Kuromon
Otebori
Otemon

Shiseien

Shinmaru

Sannomaru

Ninomaru

Hashizumemon-
tsuzukiyagura
Gokurakubashi
Sanjikkennagaya
Inuiyagura
Imoribori

Gyokusen inmaru

Tsurunomaru

Honmaru

Hishiyagura
Kahokumon
Gojikkennagaya
Hashizumemon
Hashizumebashi

Ishikawamonbashi
Ishikawamon
Ushitorayagura
Tsurunomaruzoka
Tatsumiyagura
Rikoyagura

100 m
500 ft
N

Location Kanazawa, Ishikawa prefecture
Site area 74 acres (30 ha)
Type Hirayamajiro
Layout Renkaku
Family crest Maeda

Kanazawa

Okayama Castle 1589–1597

The powerful warlord Ukita Naoie established Okayama Castle in 1573. His son Ukita Hideie, who was also an adopted son of Toyotomi Hideyoshi, began building the castle under the direction of Toyotomi in 1589. A trusted vassal, he was appointed one of Toyotomi's five senior ministers. With an annual revenue of 574,000 *koku*, Ukita was one of the most powerful *daimyo* in the late sixteenth century. However, his position changed dramatically after the Battle of Sekigahara in 1600, when he was stripped of his castle and lands and exiled to a remote island south of Edo for supporting the losing Toyotomi side.

A major reason for the western army's defeat at the Battle of Sekigahara was the defection of Kobayakawa Hideaki. Kobayakawa was Toyotomi Hideyoshi's nephew and adopted son. Before the battle, Tokugawa Ieyasu convinced Kobayakawa to switch sides, which he did, throwing the battle into confusion and securing victory for the Tokugawa. This triumph paved the way for the Tokugawa's military government to rule Japan for the next 268 years.

Kobayakawa was rewarded with Ukita Hideie's provinces of Bizen and Mimasaka, worth 550,000 *koku*. He moved into Okayama Castle in 1600. It is believed he went mad and died two years later, at 25, without an heir. His provinces were absorbed by the Ikeda clan, and Ikeda Tadatsugu, a son of Ikeda Terumasa, who was the lord of Himeji Castle, took over Okayama Castle in 1602. Tadatsugu's brother succeeded him in 1615 followed by

Below The paulownia (*kiri*) was the family crest of Toyotomi Hideyoshi. Allies such as the Ukita and Kobayakawa clans adopted this crest and it is used here on a roof ridge end tile at Okayama Castle. End tiles are called *onigawara* (monster tiles) as they often feature a threatening face. Like *shachihoko* (fish/tiger tiles), *onigawara* 'protect' the castle from misfortune.

Ikeda Mitsumasa from Tottori. Mitsumasa's successors remained at Okayama until 1869.

As lord of the rich Bizen provinces, Ukita Hideie built a castle commensurate with his large income. Beginning in 1589 and taking eight years to complete, the entire castle complex comprised 35 towers, 21 gates, a residence and garden as well as government offices. The inner enclosure was separated into two levels, the upper-level Hondan and the middle-level Nakanodan. The Tenshu and lord's residence were located in the Hondan. Government offices occupied the Nakanodan. An inner moat surrounded this enclosure on two sides. The Asahi River curved around a third. An outer moat enclosed the adjacent Ninomaru, neither of which remain.

Opposite above Topography was used to great advantage when constructing a castle to minimize costly and time-consuming earthworks. The Asahi River served as a natural moat to the north and east of Okayama Castle.

Above The Rokamon (corridor gate) was used as a passageway between the Hondan (upper enclosure) and the Omoteshoin, the feudal government office located in the Nakanodan (middle enclosure). The gate was rebuilt in concrete in 1966.

Below The seven-story black Tenshu of Okayama Castle is known as Karasujo (Crow Castle). The original Azuchi-Momoyama style structures of Okayama were destroyed by an air raid in World War II. The keep was reconstructed in concrete in 1966.

Okayama Castle's 69 ft (21 m)-high black Tenshu has a unique pentagonal shaped base. Three different-sized two-level buildings are stacked to create six levels. When viewed from outside the Hondan, the Tenshu appears to be twisted, with its roof layers out of line. A salt store attached to the central building adds to the structure's complexity. Okayama Castle is also known as U-jo (Crow Castle) because of the black timber boards lining the Tenshu, or Kinu-jo (Gold Crow Castle) because of the gilded top roof tiles.

Above The Tsukimiyagura (moon-viewing tower) from the outer enclosure. Small shooting holes at the top of the stonewall are set at intervals beneath the larger shooting holes in the plastered wall, allowing for greater gunpower at a time.

Right The Rokamon from the Nakanodan. The sloping pathway leads to the outer enclosure.

Below A round shooting hole in the *dobei* (plastered mud wall).

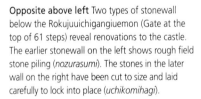

Opposite above left Two types of stonewall below the Rokujuuichigangiuemon (Gate at the top of 61 steps) reveal renovations to the castle. The earlier stonewall on the left shows rough field stone piling (*nozurasumi*). The stones in the later wall on the right have been cut to size and laid carefully to lock into place (*uchikomihagi*).

Opposite above right The Akazunomon (unopened gate) was located at the bottom of a flight of stone steps leading to the Hondan where the lord's residence and Tenshu were located. The Omoteshoin, the government office, was located in the middle-level Nakanodan. This gate was called the unopened gate because it was usually closed and a roofed passage at the northern end of the Hondan was commonly used to move between the Hondan and Nakanodan. The Akazumon, demolished in the Meiji era, was reconstructed in concrete in 1966.

POINTS OF INTEREST

The sites of many of the towers formerly in the Nakanodan of the Honmaru palace are marked to give an idea of how well fortified the castle's inner enclosure once was.

The original foundation stones of the Tenshu are laid out in the area where the Hondan once stood. These were emplaced when the Tenshu was reconstructed in concrete after its destruction by an air raid in June 1945.

The Rokujuuichigangiuemon (gate at the top of 61 steps) leads from the Hondan to the Asahi River.

The roughly piled stonewalls on the river side of the Rokujuuichi-gangiuemon clearly illustrate how stonewalls of early castles were built. They are quite different to the walls at the Rokamon (corridor gate) built 30 years later.

Okayama Castle was built at a time when feudal lords incorporated large stones into castle foundations and stonewalls as a way of showcasing their wealth. Many large stones

Right The Tsukimiyagura (moon-viewing tower) is located at the northern end of the Nakanodan. Built by Ikeda Tadakatsu in 1620, it was one of the best places for viewing the moon. Its main function however, was to protect the northwest corner of the second enclosure. The Tsukimiyagura was the only building to survive the air raid of 1945.

brought from Inujima Island can be seen at important gateways.

The small shooting holes carved out of the top stones of the walls around the Tsukimiyagura are unusual, although similar eyelets can be seen at Osaka Castle.

> **DIRECTIONS**
> A 20 minute walk or 10 minute bus ride from JR Okayama Station.

Color key on page 37

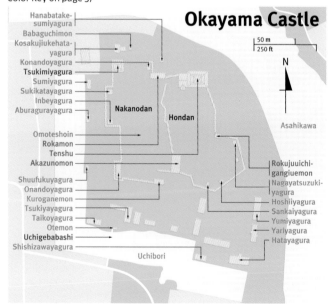

Location Okayama, Okayama prefecture
Nickname U-jo (Crow Castle, Kinu-jo (Gold Crow Castle)
Type Hirayamajiro
Layout Renkaku
Tenshu type Sotogata, Fukugoshiki (Attached)
Family crest Ukita, Kobayakawa, Ikeda

Iyo Matsuyama Castle 1602–1627

In 1602, Kato Yoshiakira began building a castle on Katsuyama on the island of Shikoku. As a samurai in Toyotomi Hideyoshi's army, Kato had distinguished himself at the Battle of Shizugatake in 1583 when he was only 20. Kato then went on to fight in many other campaigns under Toyotomi. In 1595, he was appointed lord of Masaki, with an annual income of 60,000 *koku*. After Toyotomi's death, he joined forces with the Tokugawa side at the Battle of Sekigahara. For his support he was given an income of 200,000 *koku*. Kato built a new castle at Matsuyama incorporating a number of structures from his previous castle at nearby Masaki. Accordingly, the Inuimon (northwest gate), Higashiyagura (east tower), Inuiyagura (northwest tower) and Tsutsuimon (Tsutsui gate) date from 1595. Construction continued for 24 years, but a year after completion Kato was transferred to Aizu in northern Japan. His replacement, Gamo Tadachika, died seven years later without an heir. Matsudaira Sadayuki, a member of the Tokugawa family, was next installed at the castle. Matsudaira's descendants remained at the castle until the Meiji Restoration when it was handed over to the Imperial government.

The extensive grounds of Matsuyama Castle make clever use of the natural terrain. The top of the 433 ft (132 m)-high Katsuyama hill was leveled to create the 984 ft (300 m)-long main enclosure, Honmaru. This enclosure is surrounded by 33 ft (10

Opposite above right A *renjimado* (push out window) in the Tatsumiyagura (southwest tower). Together with the Taikoyagura (drum tower) and the Taikomon (drum gate), this tower created a formidable defense against enemies who penetrated the Tsutsuimon.

Below The main Tenshu and Shotenshu (small Tenshu).

Left The central enclosure of Iyo Matsuyama Castle is a complex arrangement of towers, gates and walls. On the west are the main and small Tenshu. To the north and south are corner turrets. These four towers are connected by corridors to form an inner courtyard, similar to the Tenshu arrangement at Himeji Castle. A series of four heavily defended gates must be passed through to reach the inner enclosure. The ramp leads to the Ichinomon (first gate). The post-and-beam *koraimon* gate on the left is the Shichikimon that leads to the rear of the Honmaru.

m)-high stonewalls. Midway up the heavily forested hill is the Ninomaru, the site of the administrative quarters and lord's residence. The Sannomaru is surrounded by a moat and located at the bottom of the hill on the western side. Retainers and samurai were housed in the Sannomaru while artisans and merchants lived outside the moat to the east and west. Temples were clustered to the north. Kato encouraged the people of Masaki to move to the area by creating a tax-free commercial district.

Matsudaira Sadayuki built a new three-story Tenshu after he came to Matsuyama in 1634. A nephew of Tokugawa Ieyasu, Sadayuki was the first *shinpan* (inner circle) lord posted to this southwestern region of Japan to monitor the *tozama* ('outside' *daimyo*). Sadayuki reduced the original five-story Tenshu to three,

Above The heavily fortified Tsutuimon with the roof of the Tonashimon (doorless gate) at bottom left. Visitors could pass through the Tonashimon, then turn sharply to face the Tsutuimon. Beside the Tsutuimon is a hidden gate, the Kakuremon, from which a surprise attack could be launched.

Right Stone-dropping windows in the west wall leading to Inuimon (northwest gate) and Inui-yagura (east connecting turret of Inuimon). The Inuimon and tower defended the rear entrance to the Honmaru. The 47.5 ft (14.5 m)-long timber paneled tile roofed wall is plastered on the inside and has 10 stone-dropping windows.

Above A stone-dropping window in the Taiko-yagura. Overlooking the Tonashimon (doorless gate), drum signals were sent from this tower to warn defenders of an enemy approaching the inner enclosure of the castle.

Right Looking down from the Shotenshu (small Tenshu) at the heavily fortified Ichinomon (first gate). The small area through this gate could only accommodate a few soldiers, thus slowing down an attacking army who were then fired on from the surrounding towers. To enter the Ninomon (second gate), it was necessary to take a sharp left-hand turn.

possibly to underplay his close connections with the shogun's family, or because the foundations may have been too weak to support the original larger building. Although the main tower was reduced in size, the castle's defenses remained impressive. The approach to the Honmaru is a steep climb followed by a series of turns. Specialized entrances, such as the 'doorless gate' and 'hidden gate,' were designed to confuse invaders and provide ample opportunity for defenders to attack. Reaching the central enclosure in the north of the Honmaru, intruders passed through further heavily fortified gates to reach the courtyard, a complex of towers,

connecting corridors, gates and the main Tenshu. Ancillary courtyards with low walls, numerous shooting holes and several manned towers created yet more problems for the attackers.

The majority of the castle buildings burnt down after the castle was struck by lightning in 1784. The current complex was rebuilt in 1852. Several buildings were destroyed by air raids in 1945 and rebuilt in the 1970s.

POINTS OF INTEREST

The sophisticated defensive system of Matsuyama Castle demonstrates how far castle building techniques had advanced by the early seventeenth century. It is interesting to compare

the approach to the Honmaru of Matsuyama Castle (via the Sanno-maru and Ninomaru) with the approach to Himeji Castle. An example of the castle's unique defense is the Tonashimon (doorless gate). Situated along the approach from the Ninomaru to the Honmaru, it is thought this gate was left without a door to allow the enemy to enter and then become trapped by the well-fortified Tsutuimon around the corner. Beside the Tsutuimon is a hidden gate, Kakuremon, from which a surprise attack could be launched.

The walk to the Honmaru through the Ninomaru is steep and one can take a cable car. However, if possible,

Left and below Shooting holes and push out windows (*renjimado*) from inside the three-story main Tenshu. The town below the entire castle grounds can be seen from this vantage point.

Right The *uchibei* (inner wall) of the Shikirimon. This courtyard was built for defense of the northwest area.

descend on foot via the Ninomaru to the Sannomaru to appreciate the layout of the castle grounds.

Two *nobori ishigaki* (ascending stonewalls) of granite link the Ninomaru to the Honmaru. These sheer walls are quite rare. Folding or fan walls enclose the Honmaru.

The museum inside the castle Tenshu and subsidiary towers has an informative display of artifacts and information relating to the castle.

DIRECTIONS

From JR Matsuyama Station, it is 10 minutes by street car to Dogo Onsen. Get off at Okaido, then a 5 minute walk takes you to the cable car entrance. This takes you up to the Honmaru and back again, although it is possible to walk back down through the Ninomaru.

Color key on page 37

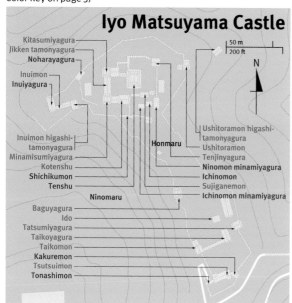

Iyo Matsuyama Castle

Kitasumiyagura
Jikken tamonyagura
Noharayagura

Inuimon
Inuiyagura

50 m
200 ft

N

Ushitoramon higashi-tamonyagura
Inuimon higashi-tamonyagura
Minamisumiyagura
Kotenshu
Shichikumon
Tenshu
Ushitoramon
Tenjinyagura
Ninomon minamiyagura
Ichinomon
Sujiganemon
Ichinomon minamiyagura

Honmaru

Ninomaru

Baguyagura
Ido
Tatsumiyagura
Taikoyagura
Taikomon
Kakuremon
Tsutsuimon
Tonashimon

Location Matsuyama, Ehime prefecture
Type Hirayamajiro
Layout Hashigokaku
Tenshu type Borogata, Renketsushiki (Compound)
Family crest Kato, Gamo, Matsudaira, Hisamatsu

Matsuyama

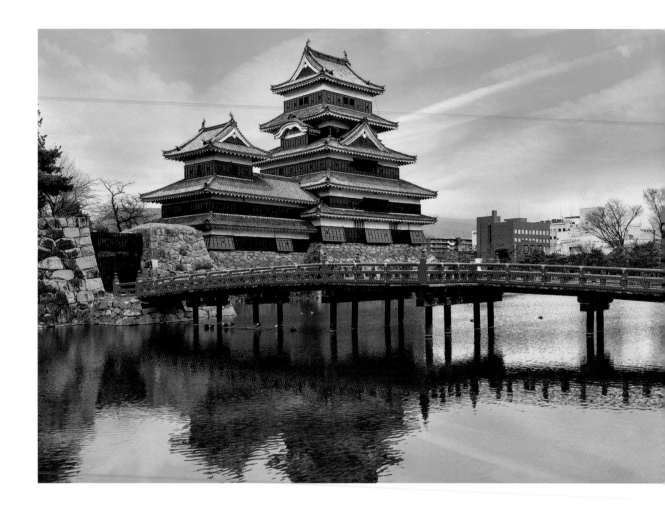

Matsumoto Castle 1590–1614

Above The 96.5 ft (29.4 m) Daitenshu (main tower) appears to have five stories from the outside but has six stories inside. The three-story Inuinokotenshu to the northwest is connected to the main tower by the Watariyagura (corridor tower) on the second level. Being one of the earlier castles and affiliated with Toyotomi Hideyoshi, Matsumoto Castle is black.

Rising dramatically against a backdrop of the Japanese Alps, Matsumoto Castle is one of Japan's most striking. Having avoided destruction in the wars of the late sixteenth century, the Meiji Restoration in the nineteenth century and the air raids of World War II, Matsumoto Castle is one of the oldest original castles in Japan.

The site of Matsumoto Castle was first used in 1504 as a sub-fort of the Ogasawara clan. Initially called Fukashi, it was renamed Matsumoto in 1582 by Ogasawara Sadayoshi. In 1590, Toyotomi Hideyoshi awarded Ishikawa Kazumasa the domain of Shinano, which included Matsumoto Castle. Ishikawa planned to rebuild the castle but died before work began, leaving construction to his eldest son, Yasunaga.

Six different families occupied Matsumoto Castle between 1590 and 1869: Ishikawa (1590–1613), Ogasawara (1613–17), Toda (1617–33) and again from 1726 to 1869, Matsudaira (1633–38), Hotta (1638–42) and Mizuno (1642–1725). The family crests of these lords adorn roof tiles at various points on the castle.

Matsumoto Castle is a flat land floating castle (*ukishiro*). The Uchibori (inner moat) surrounds the Honmaru (main enclosure) where the Tenshu complex and Honmarugoten (palace) are located. The lord of Matsumoto lived in the Honmarugoten and ran his government headquarters from here.

Left Rising directly from the moat, Matsumoto Castle is an *ukishiro* (floating castle). The rough piling of the Tenshu base is less sophisticated than castles built in the following 20 years, which saw great advances in stonewall construction techniques.

Center left Completely open on the east and south sides, the Tsukimiyagura (moon-viewing tower) was built for the popular pastime of moon viewing. The Tsukimiyagura and Tatsuminotsuke-yagura (east keep) were built around 1634 by Matsudaira Naomasa (1601–66). Matsudaira occupied the castle for five years (1633–38) during which time a rice granary and stable for 54 horses were constructed.

Below Originally built in 1595, the Taikomon (drum gate) was torn down at the beginning of the Meiji era (1868–1912) and rebuilt in 1999. A *taiko* drum announced the time, the arrival of visitors and signaled emergencies from this gate. *Taiko* were also used in battle to send commands, directives and communiqués.

The Ninomaru (second enclosure) formed a U shape around the Honmaru and was also enclosed by a moat. The Ninomaru palace (Kosanji-goten), various storehouses and a rice granary were located here. The two inner enclosures were enclosed by the Sannomaru (third enclosure), where about 90 important samurai were housed. The 1.4 mile (2.2 km)-long Sotobori (outer moat) surrounded the entire castle, accessed by four crossing points to the Sannomaru.

Matsumoto Castle has a complex Tenshu arrangement comsisting of a five-story Tenshu connected to a small tower to the northwest by the Watari-yagura (corridor-style tower) and a moon-viewing tower to the south. The complex Tenshu arrangement at Matsumoto was rare for castles of the 1590s, which usually had only a single main tower.

According to legend, a curse was placed on the castle by a peasant called Kasuke in 1686. Protesting a

tax increase, Kasuke led a failed uprising against the lord of the castle. He was captured and sentenced to death. On the day of his execution, Kasuke glared in resentment at the castle and from that day on it began to lean. By the early twentieth century, the lean was so bad that a rope was tied around the main pillar on the fourth floor and pulled through the window to straighten the structure. This method appeared to have worked as the castle now stands tall, albeit with rope marks ingrained on the pillar.

The castle was almost demolished in the Meiji period (1868–1912) when the emperor was restored to power. Happily, it was saved from destruction by local citizens who raised funds to buy and restore it in 1911. The castle was designated a Historic Site in 1930, the Tenshu a National Treasure in 1936.

POINTS OF INTEREST

Rope marks on the central pillar inside the main Tenshu.

The rare round pillars inside the Tenshu.

Different family crests on the roof tiles around the castle.

Above A sense of opulence is created with minimal materials and color through pattern, proportion and craftsmanship. The carved wooden ornament at the apex of the roof gable is called a *gengyo*. Meaning 'to pour water on,' *gengyo* were also used in temple architecture as a protective charm against fire.

Right The Taikomon from inside the Honmaru.

Far right A-bell shaped window (*katomado*) in the Daitenshu.

Color key on page 37

DIRECTIONS

A 15 minute walk from Matsumoto Station.

Below left An *ishiotoshimado* (stone-dropping window) in the Inuikotenshu (north small tower).

Below The Daitenshu is connected to the Tsukimiyagura (moon-viewing tower) by the Tatsumitsukeyagura. The Honmaru is surrounded by the Uchibori (inner moat), and the Ninomaru forms a U shape around this. The Nakabori surrounded the Ninomaru which was, in turn, surrounded by the Sannomaru and Sotobori (outer moat).

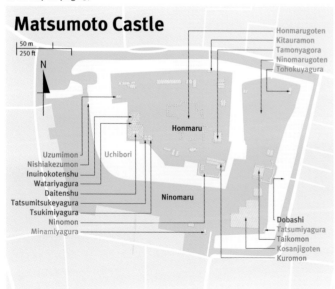

Matsumoto Castle

50 m
250 ft

N

Uzumimon
Nishiakezumon
Inuinokotenshu
Watariyagura
Daitenshu
Tatsumitsukeyagura
Tsukimiyagura
Ninomon
Minamiyagura

Uchibori

Honmaru

Ninomaru

Honmarugoten
Kitauramon
Tamonyagura
Ninomarugoten
Tohokuyagura

Dobashi
Tatsumiyagura
Taikomon
Kosanjigoten
Kuromon

Location Matsumoto, Nagano prefecture
Nickname Fukashi, Karasu-jo (Crow Castle)
Type Ukashiro or Hirajiro
Layout Donshinen
Tenshu type Sotogata, Renritsushiki (Compound)
Family crests Ishikawa, Ogasawara, Matsudaira, Mizuno, Toda, Toyotomi

Matsumoto

Matsue Castle 1607–1611

A law was passed in 1607 forbidding young girls to dance in the streets of Matsue, a small town on the west coast of Japan. Lafcadio Hearn, nineteenth-century writer and Matsue resident, explained that whenever any maiden danced, the castle hill, Oshiroyama, would shudder and the entire building would quiver. It did so because a beautiful young girl had been buried alive under the castle walls as a sacrifice to the gods.

All that is known of her was that she loved to dance.

Horio Yoshiharu established Matsue Castle in 1607. Horio had been a vassal of Oda Nobunaga and Toyotomi Hideyoshi, but sided with Tokugawa Ieyasu at the Battle of Sekigahara in 1600. He was rewarded with the provinces of Izumo and Oki. Horio initially governed from Toda Castle in Hirose until the mountain castle could no longer accommodate

the administrative needs of the growing castle town. His next castle at Matsue was closer to sea transportation and less susceptible to flooding. Completed in 1611, it was occupied by three generations of the Horio family. Matsue Castle was subsequently passed to Kyogoku Tadataka, who ruled from 1634 to 1638. Like Horio, he had no successor, so control of the castle was handed to Matsudaira Naomasa, Tokugawa Ieyasu's grand-

Left Four bridges over the Uchibori (inner moat) allow access to the inner enclosures.

Below left At 98 ft (30 m), the Tenshu at Matsue Castle is the third tallest original one in Japan after Himeji and Matsumoto. The castle is also known as Chidori-jo (Plover Castle) due to the shape of the *irimoyahafu* (roof gables) that resemble the outstretched wings of the plover bird. The castle has 95 small secret outlets for guns in the walls and a narrow outlet over the attached portico entrance to thrust spears onto intruders.

Below The main entrance to the castle is through the basement, which is sealed with an iron door. A 79 ft (24 m)-deep well in the basement supplied the castle with water in the event of a siege. Rice, salt and dried goods were also stored here.

Above The interior of the castle is quite dark, with minimal openings to admit light. The timber construction makes the castle susceptible to fire. Unique to Matsue Castle, the stairs are made of paulownia timber, which does not burn easily. This meant occupants could escape via the stairs in the case of fire.

son. Naomasa was transferred from Matsumoto Castle in Shinano province, and ten generations of his family ruled Izumo from Matsue Castle for the next 230 years.

The black wooden Tenshu of Matsue Castle is one of the 12 original Tenshu remaining in Japan. Although well fortified, the castle was never attacked and was fortunate to escape lightning strikes, the primary reason many castles were destroyed during the Edo period. The 98 ft (30 m)-high Tenshu appears to have five stories from the outside but has six internal floors, a basement and an older style *borogata* watchtower. The 24.6 ft (7.5 m)-high stone base is vertical, indicative of the older style of *gobozumi* wall piling. Long stones are embedded deep into the wall, with the larger surface of the stones facing inward to form a solid base. This type of piling is also used at the base of the Tenshu at Hikone Castle.

Stone-dropping windows guard each side of the portico-style entrance, which is sealed with a steel door. Small stones could be taken out of the wall and thrown through the stone-dropping windows without compromising the wall's stability. Spears could be thrust through a narrow oblong opening above the entrance at unwelcome visitors. Black timber boards line the walls of the Tenshu. Made of chestnut wood donated by local farmers, the poor quality timber was painted with persimmon juice to protect it from insects. More economical than white plastered walls, Matsue's black walls are also more suited to the local climate, which has high humidity in summer, heavy snowfalls in winter and typhoons in early autumn. Two *shachihoko* (fish-like creatures) made of wood and covered with bronze 'protect' the roof ridge. At 7.4 ft (2.25 m) high, they are second in size only to Nagoya Castle's famous gold-plated *shachihoko*.

Many of the castle buildings were demolished on the orders of the Imperial government during the Meiji Restoration. The Tenshu was sold to a wreaking company in 1875 for a minor sum but repurchased by local residents to save it from destruction. The Tenshu was renovated between 1950 and 1955. A number of towers have recently been reconstructed.

POINTS OF INTEREST

The feudal lord of Matsue maintained around 3,000 samurai retainers—warriors in war and bureaucrats in peacetime. Their residences were located around the castle grounds. Many *buke yashiki* (samurai houses) can be visited in the samurai quarter today. The castle town of Matsue was laid out with merchants on the north bank of the Ohashi River and artisans on the south bank. Temples in the south could be turned into an armed camp in the event of war. A settlement for gunnery troops in the south formed the first line of defence for the city and castle.

DIRECTIONS

From JR Matsue Station the bus to Matsue jo Otemae takes 10 minutes. Alternatively, it is a 20 minute walk to the castle.

Above The inside of the *dobei* are plastered and the shooting holes timber-lined. The tile roof provides protection from weather and gunfire.

Top The Minamiyagura (south turret). There were ten towers located on the walls surrounding the castle. Soldiers could run along corridors between the turrets. This tower was reconstructed in 2001 along with the Nakayagura (inner tower) and Taikoyagura (drum tower).

Above Timber-lined *dobei* (mud walls) with shooting holes run along the stonewalls rising from the moat.

Right Minamiyagura and Naka-yagura. The Taikoyagura is in the distance. The Uchibori (inner moat) surrounds the inner enclosures, the Honmaru and Ninomaru. The inner and outer moats are fed by nearby Lake Shinji.

Far left The stairs at Matsue Castle are made of paulownia wood. Paulownia is very light and difficult to burn. In war it was possible to lift the stairs to impede an advancing enemy and in fire it was possible to exit via them. Each step is 4 in (10 cm) thick and 5 ft (1.6 m) wide.

Left *Renjimado* (push out windows).

Above The base of the Tenshu is in the *gobozumi* style where long stones are embedded deep into the wall. Although the stones appear to be stacked randomly, their length and careful placement ensure a very stable wall.

Color key on page 37

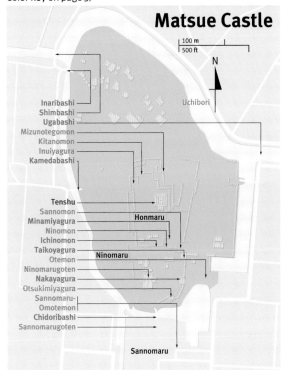

Matsue Castle

| 100 m |
| 500 ft |

N

Inaribashi
Shimbashi
Ugabashi
Mizunotegomon
Kitanomon
Inuiyagura
Kamedabashi

Uchibori

Tenshu
Sannomon
Minamiyagura
Ninomon
Ichinomon
Taikoyagura
Otemon
Ninomarugoten
Nakayagura
Otsukimiyagura
Sannomaru-
Omotemon
Chidoribashi
Sannomarugoten

Honmaru

Ninomaru

Sannomaru

Location Matsue, Shimane prefecture
Nickname Chidori-jo (Plover Castle)
Type Hirayamajiro
Layout Hashigokoku
Tenshu type Borogata, Fukugoshiki (Attached)
Family crest Horio, Kyogoku, Matsudaira

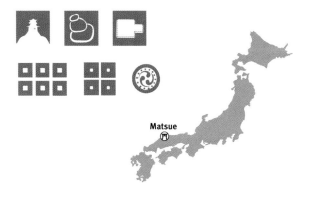

Matsue

Kochi Castle 1601–1603

Just prior to the Battle of Sekigahara in 1600, Chiyo, the wife of Yamauchi Katsutoyo (1545–1605), sent her husband a letter concealed in the chin strap of a messenger's hat. Yamauchi was a vassal who had served under Oda Nobunaga and Toyotomi Hideyoshi. The letter relayed vital information about Toyotomi loyalist forces and suggested her husband switch allegiances. Fortuitously, Katsutoyo took her advice and fought on the winning Tokugawa side. In recognition of his service, Katsutoyo was made first lord of the province of Tosa in 1600. He began constructing Kochi Castle the following year. Located on Otakasaka hill, the main buildings were built within two years and the whole castle complex was completed by 1611. Sixteen consecutive generations of the Yamauchi family ruled Tosa over the following 270 years. Today, in recognition of her wisdom, a bronze statue of Chiyo watches over the approach to the main citadel.

Before Yamauchi Katsutoyo arrived in 1600, Tosa was ruled by the warlord Chosokabe Motochika. Chosokabe had arrived in 1588 and built a castle on Otakasaka (Otaka hill), replacing the original watchtower and mud ramparts erected on the site in the fourteenth century by the rural warrior, Otaka Matsumaru. Chosokabe abandoned this site soon after due to flooding and moved to Urado. As retribution for supporting the Toyotomi side at the Battle of Sekigahara, Chosokabe was stripped of his castle, lands and revenue of 222,000 *koku*. When Yamauchi

Left Lying 145 ft (44.4 m) above sea level, the 60.7 ft (18.5 m)-high Tenshu appears to have four stories but actually has six levels inside. In the *borogata* style, it has a watchtower on top with an exterior walkway. Iron spikes, known as 'ninja repellants,' run around the castle above the top of the stone base. A unique feature are warrior windows (*mushamado*). These horizontal slat windows in the low plastered walls (*dobei*) surrounding the Honmaru provided lookouts for samurai.

Below The two-story Otemon (main gate) of Kochi Castle was originally built around 1610 and rebuilt in 1664. It is a box-style gate (*masugatamon*). The main pillars are made of zelkova and reinforced with copper plates. The gate is oriented so that it is not possible to see into the castle grounds. The Otemon survived the fire of 1727, making it one of the oldest structures at the castle.

Katsutoyo came to Tosa he undertook works to prevent the flooding and built Kochi Castle on Otakasaka in 1601. Destroyed by fire in 1727, most of the castle was rebuilt in 1753. Following the Meiji Restoration, the castle and grounds were redeveloped into a prefectural park, saving the buildings from demolition. Fifteen of the remaining buildings have been designated Important National Cultural Assets. The whole area is designated a Historic Site.

Above The Higashitamon, Tsumemon and Rokamon. The Higashitamon (east corridor) leads from the Tenshu to the Tsumemon (guardroom or 'trick gate'), so-called because it did not lead to the next enclosure at ground level as it appears to, confusing intruders who would be attacked by guards when they reached this dead end. To access the next enclosure, the Ninomaru, it was necessary to turn right and ascend the stairs. The Tsumemon would then take one to the Honmaru (inner enclosure) where the lord's reception suite (Seiren) and Tenshu were located. The lord's palace (Goten) was located in the Ninomaru, but was destroyed by fire in 1727, along with many of the other castle buildings.

POINTS OF INTEREST

The arrangement of buildings within the Honmaru is unique to Kochi Castle. Honmarugoten or Seiren, the lord's reception rooms, are adjacent to the main citadel or Tenshu. These

Left The box-shaped area in front of the Otemon is surrounded by stonewalls topped with low timber walls. Samurai could fire upon intruders from the protection of these walls.

Right Unique to Kochi Castle is the lord's reception suite, the Seiren, attached to the Tenshu (behind). It consists of a guardroom, an entrance hall and several other chambers. The floor of the main chamber is raised for the lord to sit on when receiving guests. On the west side is a small room where warriors hid should they be needed to protect the lord.

Above Nail coverings (kugikakushi) at the Otemon are often called breast ironware (chichikanamono) because of their resemblance to the female breast.

Right A copper-plated shachihoko on the roof ridge of the Tenshu.

buildings were usually located in lesser enclosures, such as the Ninomaru. Although the Tenshu is a separate building that can be isolated in the event of fire by closing the thick, plastered doors, it is possible to step directly from the Honmaruseiren into the Tenshu. The Higashitamon is also located beside the Tenshu, allowing movement through a series of corridor towers enclosing the Honmaru without stepping outside.

Although the layout of the compounds of Kochi Castle appears straightforward, with the main enclosure at the highest point and the second and third enclosures

descending down the hill, the approach to the castle is deceptive. After passing through the Tetsumon (iron gate), and turning to the left to go up the flight of stone steps, the path to the Ninomaru was hidden behind walls lined with shooting holes. Invaders had no choice but to proceed straight ahead toward the Tsumemon (guardroom or 'trick gate'). Built over a waterless moat connecting the Honmaru and Ninomaru, the entrance was called a trick gate because an enemy who succeeded in breaking through would end up in a square outside the main citadel. Entry was only possible from the Ninomaru,

which required a right turn before reaching the Tsumemon.

Metal spikes line the top of the stonewalls for extra defense. Slatted windows (mushamado) in the plastered mud walls (dobei) gave soldiers in the Honmaru an excellent view over the castle grounds. Stone gutters protrude from the walls to channel Kochi's high rainfall away from the foundations to prevent the walls weakening. Letters engraved on the stones lining the walls, to the left of the Otemon (main gate), represent individuals involved in the construction of the castle.

Kochi Castle is particularly attractive because of its contrasting black walls and white trim, black gates and white plastered walls, decorative monster end tiles (onigawara), copper 'dolphin' tiles (shachihoko) and roofing arrangements of dormer gables (chidorihafu) and undulating gables (karahafu).

DIRECTIONS

Kochi City is situated in the south of the island of Shikoku. Taking two and a half hours by train from Okayama, the journey through the mountains and alongside the gorges of Shikoku is spectacular. The castle is a 10 minute taxi ride or 20 minute walk from Kochi Station.

Above Iron plating with copper nail coverings on the door of the Otemon.

Below left The timber lattice of the window in the Higashitamon is plastered for fireproofing. The rain door (*amado*) could be slid across for further protection. This corridor tower leads from the Tenshu to the Tsumemon.

Below The lord's reception suite was built in the *shoin* style with *tatami* matting and *shoji* and *fusuma* (thick paper screens) dividing rooms. Ornately carved transoms above the horizontal beam above the screens (*nageshi*) allow airflow when the *fusuma* are shut.

Color key on page 37

Kochi Castle

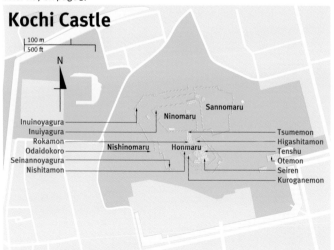

100 m
500 ft
N

Inuinoyagura
Inuiyagura
Rokamon
Odaidokoro
Seinannoyagura
Nishitamon

Nishinomaru
Honmaru
Ninomaru
Sannomaru

Tsumemon
Higashitamon
Tenshu
Otemon
Seiren
Kuroganemon

Location Kochi, Kochi prefecture
Site area 32 acres (13 ha)
Type Hirayamajiro
Layout Hashigokoku
Tenshu type Borogata, Dokuritsushiki (Independent)
Family crest Yamauchi

Kochi

Bitchu-Matsuyama Castle 1575, 1683

Situated 1,411 ft (430 m) above sea level, Bitchu-Matsuyama is Japan's highest surviving castle. From its vantage point on heavily forested Mt Gagyu, the castle commands the surrounding area.

A fort was first constructed in the area in 1240 by Akiba Saburo Shigenobu. When Mimura Motochika became the feudal lord of the region in the late sixteenth century, that stronghold was enlarged to encompass the castle's current site. With the help of the Mori clan, Mimura conquered the entire Bitchu area, but was later forced from the castle after betraying the Mori. In 1600, Kobori Masatsugu and his son Masakazu came to the area on orders of the Tokugawa shogunate. They were succeeded by Mizunoya Katsutaka in 1681, who rebuilt the Tenshu, towers and gates and built the Onegoya, an administrative building, on the southern side of the mountain. In 1744, Itakura Katsuzumi became lord of the castle and was subsequently followed by eight Itakura lords through 126 years.

Bitchu-Matsuyama is a small castle with an original two-story Tenshu, several reconstructed towers and original plastered mud walls (*dobei*). Its appeal lies in its location on the peak of Mt Gagyu, with stunning views over the surrounding mountains. The castle makes interesting use of the topography, with the stonewalls and tower bases appearing to grow organically out of the natural rock.

Opposite below At 1,410 ft (430 m) above sea level and surrounded by mountains, the isolation of Bitchu-Matsuyama rendered large castle buildings unnecessary. The two-story black and white Tenshu, although small, has a commanding view of the surrounding area. The towers surrounding the Honmaru are protected by fan-shaped stone-dropping windows at their corners, as seen on the Gonohirayagura (fifth one-level tower) in the foreground. The undulating roof (*karahafu*) of the stone-dropping window of the Tenshu adds to the beauty of this remote castle.

Left Shooting holes in the plastered mud walls (*dobei*) atop the stonewall.

Below The natural topography has been used ingeniously to create a labyrinth-like approach to the Honmaru, the highest point of the castle. The hill has been carved, then faced with stone, creating walls and steps. Natural stone and rock face are incorporated into this design.

The current Tenshu dates from the renovation by Mizunoya Katsutaka in 1681. Quite compact, it is dominated by a large stone-dropping window (*ishiotoshimado*) at its center with an undulating roof gable(*karahafu*). Slatted windows surround the walls, and a gabled roof (*irimoyahafu*), its sides extending to the edges of the roof, sits atop the second level. The walls are a combination of black timber paneling and white plaster.

At the rear of the castle, past the Mizunotemon gate ruins, are the Bansho enclosure and terraced enclosures called the Aihatakekido Ruins. These lead to the Tenjin enclosures, the ruins of an outlying fort that formed part of the castle's northern defenses. A further 656 ft (200 m) along are the earthwork ruins of the original Oomatsuyama Castle dating to 1240.

The order to abolish castles early in the Meiji era (1868–1912) left Bitchu-Matsuyama Castle in ruins. A citizen's group was formed in 1929 to preserve the castle and repair the tower. Further restoration and repairs

Right Natural terrain has been used to great effect at Bitchu-Matsuyama, with the Tenshu, walls and towers rising from the sheer rock face. The Nijuyagura (two-story tower) appears to grow out of the rock.

have continued under Takahashi City. Bitchu-Matsuyama Castle was designated an Important Cultural Property in 1950. Two towers, four gates and some mud walls were reconstructed in 1995.

POINTS OF INTEREST

Bitchu-Matsuyama has one of the 12 original Tenshu remaining in Japan. Its small, squat shape and appearance of growing out of the rocky outcrop make it an interesting addition to this group of surviving Tenshu.

The effort required to reach this castle reveals how inaccessible mountain castles were. The isolation, interesting buildings and stunning view, however, are well worth the effort.

DIRECTIONS

Located in Takahashi, Okayama prefecture, the train from Okayama takes about one hour. From Takahashi Station take a taxi halfway up the mountain to the car park and then walk up to the castle site. It is possible to walk back to the town from the castle in about 1.5 hours.

Below left The Gonohirayagura (fifth one-level tower) and the Rokunohirayagura (sixth one-level tower) flank the gateway to the Honmaru.

Below Steps leading to the Gonohira-yagura.

Color key on page 37

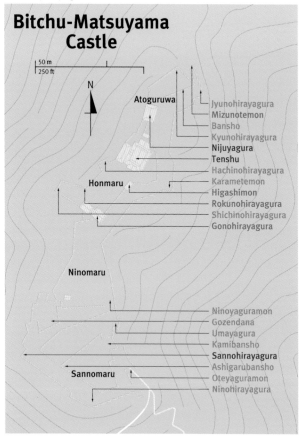

Bitchu-Matsuyama Castle

50 m
250 ft

N

Atoguruwa

Jyunohirayagura
Mizunotemon
Bansho
Kyunohirayagura
Nijuyagura
Tenshu
Hachinohirayagura
Karametemon
Higashimon
Rokunohirayagura
Shichinohirayagura
Gonohirayagura

Honmaru

Ninomaru

Ninoyaguramon
Gozendana
Umayagura
Kamibansho
Sannohirayagura
Ashigarubansho
Oteyaguramon
Ninohirayagura

Sannomaru

Location Takahashi, Okayama prefecture
Nickname Takahashi
Type Yamajiro
Layout Renkaku
Tenshu type Fukugoshiki (Attached)
Family crest Mizunoya, Itakura

Bitchu Matsuyama

Top The Tenshu and *dobei* with round and rectangular shooting holes.

Above The Higashimon (east gate) is the side gate leading to the Honmaru.

Inuyama Castle
1535, 1601–1620

On a hill overlooking the Kiso River, Inuyama Castle commanded the border between Owari and Mino provinces. Established in 1535 by Oda Nobuyasu, the uncle of Oda Nobunaga, its strategic position in central Honshu saw it play an important role in the events leading up to the unification of Japan during the Warring States period (1477–1575).

Prior to the Komaki campaign in 1584, Ikeda Terumasa took the castle for his lord, Toyotomi Hideyoshi, giving Toyotomi a strategic advantage over his rival, Tokugawa Ieyasu. Tokugawa subsequently retreated, leaving Toyotomi to rule Japan until his death in 1598. Ikeda Terumasa later formed an alliance with Tokugawa Ieyasu by marrying his second daughter. He fought on the Tokugawa side at the Battle of Sekigahara in 1600, for which he was rewarded with the province of Harima and Himeji Castle.

Inuyama Castle's 62 ft (19 m)-high Tenshu is one of the most handsome of the 12 surviving Tenshu in Japan. Its watchtower affords a superb view over the river and surrounding countryside. From the exterior there appears to be three levels, but inside there are four, plus another two within the stone base. The first floor contains a guardroom, two storage rooms and living quarters for the lord. Warriors would hide in the rear of the room to protect their lord from danger. The second floor has shelves on three walls to store weapons. Bell-shaped windows (*katomado*) and a mix of undulating gables (*karahafu*, *kirizumahafu* and *irimoyahafu*) add to the beauty of the black and white Tenshu.

There is some disagreement as to when and where Inuyama Castle's

Above A concrete reconstruction of the Honmarumon (gate) leading to the Honmaru (main enclosure). The Tenshu and stonewalls are the only original buildings left at Inuyama Castle. Most of the other buildings were torn down when the Meiji government took possession in 1871. A major earthquake in 1891 wrought further destruction.

Below The Kiso River as viewed from the Tenshu. Windows comprise a sliding *shoji* screen to admit light and keep out drafts, timber slats and timber shutter doors.

Above The strategic location of Inuyama Castle beside the Kiso River in central Honshu made this a hotly contested site in the late sixteenth century. As such, the castle changed hands more than once between Tokugawa and Toyotomi loyalists. In 1617, after a succession of lords, the Naruse clan moved in and remained at the castle until it was taken from them by the new Meiji government in 1871. They then retook possession in 1895, making Inuyama the only privately owned castle in Japan for many years.

Far left The older *borogata*-style Tenshu has a watchtower affording stunning views of the surrounding landscape. Appearing as three levels, there are four levels inside the Tenshu, with another two in the stone base.

Left The timber eaves are thickly plastered to protect against fire. Windows push outwards and shooting holes remain closed until needed.

Left Looking at the Honmaru from the Tenshu. The two-story building in the middle is the reconstructed Honmarumon gate.

Below Leaving the castle down the steep hill between the Honmarumon and the Kuromon.

Opposite above The stone piling used at Inuyama is *nozurazumi*, the most basic and oldest style of stonewall construction. Field stones are piled roughly, limiting the height and gradient of the wall.

Below left The uppermost room on the fourth floor of the Tenshu is called the Kooran (high rails room). With a 360-degree view from the surrounding veranda, this room was used as a lookout. The black *katomado* (flower window) is not a functioning window. Such attention to aesthetics reveals the castle was much more than a fortress.

Below right An 11.8 ft (3.6 m)-wide corridor surrounds the central inner rooms on the first and second floors of the Tenshu. These corridors are called *mushabashiri* (warriors running) and were wide enough to accommodate a number of fast-moving warriors in a time of attack. The central room on the first floor was divided into a guardroom, two storage rooms and the Jodannoma, which had a raised floor and was used as living quarters for Lord Naruse when he was staying at the castle. Weapons were stored in the inner room on the second floor.

Tenshu was built. Some believe that the Tenshu was originally built at Kanayama Castle, further up the Kiso River, in 1537, dismantled in 1599 and shipped to its present site. This would make Inuyama Castle the oldest surviving Tenshu in Japan. The old-style *borogata* watchtower on top of the Tenshu supports this theory. Restoration work carried out in the 1960s, however, suggests that the Tenshu was built between 1601 and 1620.

A succession of lords, comprising the Oda, Ikeda, Nakagawa, Nagao and Ogasawara, resided at Inuyama until 1617. The Naruse clan then took possession and remained at the castle until it was taken from them in 1871.

At this time, all the structures except the Tenshu were destroyed.

The castle was returned to the Naruse family in 1895 on the condition that the damage wrought by the Great Nobi Earthquake of 1891 was repaired. For many years it was the only privately owned castle in Japan, until recently, when it was sold to the city of Inuyama and taken over by Aichi prefecture.

POINTS OF INTEREST
The stunning location of the castle's handsome Tenshu on the hill overlooking the Kiso River.

The original Tenshu.

The view from the watchtower.

Color key on page 37

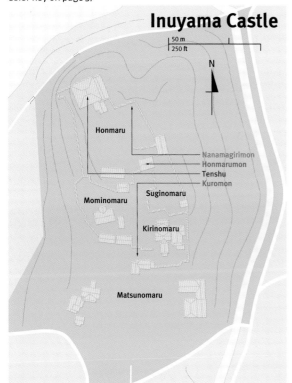

Inuyama Castle

50 m
250 ft

N

Honmaru
Nanamagirimon
Honmarumon
Tenshu
Kuromon
Mominomaru
Suginomaru
Kirinomaru
Matsunomaru

DIRECTIONS
A 15 minute walk from Inuyama Yuen Station.

Location Inuyama, Aichi prefecture
Nickname Hakutei
Type Hirayamajiro
Layout Hashigokoku
Tenshu type Borogata, Fukugohsiki (Attached)
Family crest Oda, Naruse

Inuyama

Hiroshima Castle 1589–1599

Hiroshima Castle was established by Mori Terumoto in 1589. One of the wealthiest and most powerful *daimyo* in Japan, Mori ruled his nine provinces that today comprise Hiroshima, Shimane, Yamaguchi and parts of Tottori and Okayama prefectures from there.

Mori's power lay in the west of Japan. His support was crucial to Oda Nobunaga in his quest to unify Japan in the late sixteenth century. Toyotomi Hideyoshi was responsible for gaining the support of the western provinces for Oda, a task that took five years to accomplish from his base at Himeji Castle. He eventually gained Mori Terumoto's allegiance after the water siege of Takamatsu Castle in 1582.

Mori became one of Toyotomi's trusted vassals and was appointed one of five regents to govern Japan in the name of Hideyoshi's son, Hideyori, upon Toyotomi Hideyoshi's death. Mori supported the Toyotomi loyalists during the Battle of Sekigahara in 1600, but did not take part in the battle. As punishment for taking the wrong side, he was forced to cede most of his territory and his income was cut from 1,200,000 *koku* to 360,000 *koku*. He was sent to the remote coastal town of Hagi where he established a new castle.

Hiroshima Castle was given to Fukushima Masanori of Kiyosu, another ally of Toyotomi Hideyoshi. After floods damaged the castle in

1617, Fukushima sought permission from the Tokugawa shogunate to repair the castle. After waiting two years without a reply, he went ahead. As punishment for altering the castle without permission, he was removed to the less profitable province of Kawanakajima in Nagano. Hiroshima Castle and the eight Bingo counties were then passed to Asano Nagaakira. Twelve generations of the Asano family then held this position for 250 years until the Meiji Restoration in 1868.

Following the abolition of feudal domains and the establishment of prefectures in 1871, the castle served as a military facility. It was designated a National Treasure in 1931 but was destroyed by the atomic bomb in

Opposite above A watchtower on the fifth level of the 85 ft (26 m)-high Tenshu gives vantage over the surrounding area. As a flatland castle, height was crucial. The main tower, plus the base, is 125 ft (38 m) tall.

Above left Entry to the Ninomaru (second enclosure) is via the Ninomaruomotemon. The Hirayagura (one-level tower) is on the right of the gate.

Above The stone piling of the 39 ft (12 m)-high Tenshu base is quite rough, indicating that Hiroshima Castle was built toward the beginning of the major castle building period of 1576–1615.

Left The Ninomaruomotemon (front gate to the second enclosure) was reconstructed in 1991 using traditional materials and construction methods.

Below The Tamonyagura (long tower) and the two-level Taikoyagura (drum tower) line the stonewall surrounding the Honmaru (inner enclosure). A drum was kept here to sound the hour and send signals. The Uchibori (inner moat) surrounds the Honmaru.

Right Inside the Ninomaru-omotemon.

Below The Tenshu was reconstructed in concrete in 1958 after the original was destroyed by the atomic bomb on August 6, 1945.

Opposite Originally covering an extensive area, Hiroshima Castle was surrounded by three moats and the Otagawa River to the west. After the Meiji Restoration in 1868, the outer and middle moats were filled in and now most of the original castle grounds are occupied by city buildings. The remaining Uchibori (inner moat), Honmaru and Ninomaru were designated a National Historic Site in 1953.

1945. The Tenshu was reconstructed in concrete in 1958 and is now a museum housing artifacts of Hiroshima and the original castle.

POINTS OF INTEREST

An Obikuruwa surrounds the Honmaru at Hiroshima Castle. This is a narrow enclosure that encircles a larger enclosure. It is named after an *obi*, the waistband worn around a *kimono*.

The foundations of the east and south-connected keeps seen beside the reconstructed independent Tenshu give an idea of the original Tenshu's form.

Hiroshima is a black castle. Many castles built before 1600 were finished in a black lacquer made from pine resin, black ink (*sumi*) and Japanese lacquer. This protects the timber from the elements and insect infestation.

DIRECTIONS

Hiroshima City is on the main Shinkansen Line. The castle is 10 minutes by bus or tram from JR Hiroshima Station. Get off at Kamiya cho, then it is a 15 minute walk to the castle.

Color key on page 37

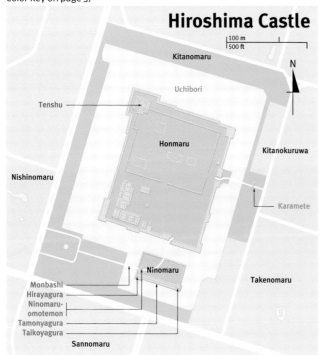

Hiroshima Castle

| 100 m |
| 500 ft |

Kitanomaru

N

Uchibori

Tenshu

Honmaru

Kitanokuruwa

Nishinomaru

Karamete

Ninomaru

Takenomaru

Monbashi
Hirayagura
Ninomaru-
omotemon
Tamonyagura
Taikoyagura

Sannomaru

Location Hiroshima, Hiroshima prefecture
Nickname Rijo
Type Hirajiro
Layout Renkaku
Tenshu type Borogata, Fukugoshiki (Attached)
Family crest Mori, Fukushima, Asano

Hiroshima

Marugame Castle 1587

Perched on top of Kameyama hill on the island of Shikoku, Marugame Castle overlooks the Bingonada Sea to the main island of Honshu. First used by the Nara clan during the Muromachi period (1338–1573), the site now houses the remains of the castle established in 1587 by warlord Ikoma Chikamasa. After building another castle at nearby Takamatsu, Chikamasa handed Marugame Castle to his son, Ikoma Kazumasa, who turned it into a formidable stronghold. Kazumasa was unable to remain at the castle, however, due to the Tokugawa shogunate's *Ikkoku ichijo rei* law of 1615, which restricted *daimyo* to one castle per province. Marugame Castle was dismantled in 1615.

The castle was given new life in 1641 when a small part of western Sanuki was given to Yamazaki Ieharu for bravery during the 1638 Shimabara Rebellion. Yamazaki's new fief included the site of Marugame Castle, which he rebuilt between 1641 and 1644. It is believed that most of the stonewalls date from this time. Fourteen years later, the castle was passed to the Kyogoku clan, who further improved it by adding the Otemon complex. The Kyogoku clan remained at Marugame Castle until the Meiji Restoration. Fire razed many of the buildings in 1869 before the Imperial government destroyed much of what remained the following year.

Marugame Castle utilizes the natural rocky terrain of Kameyama as its foundation. The Honmaru and

Top The Oteninomon is a post-and-beam (*koraimon*) gate. Upon passing through, you enter a courtyard and turn right to go through the Oteichinomon, a two-story *yaguramon*.

Above The Kyogoku clan controlled the castle for over 200 years (1658–1868). Their family crest can be found on end tiles throughout the castle grounds.

Below left Marugame is a three-level *sotogata*-style Tenshu. Small but beautifully proportioned, its vantage point 217 ft (66 m) above sea level negated the need for multiple levels.

Below The Oteichinomon was constructed by the Kyogoku family, who came to the castle around 1658.

Tenshu are positioned on the highest point of the hill, which is carved to create successive descending enclosures. Enclosures at the base of the mountain house the palace, gardens, riding grounds and main gate. Chief retainers' mansions were located at the front and rear entrances to the castle and samurai houses in the inner area of the outer moat (filled in during the Meiji era). Today, the three-level

Tenshu is one of only 12 original Tenshu remaining in Japan. The Otemon, originally built in 1670, and the Tenshu were restored in 1950.

POINTS OF INTEREST
The area around the Genkansakigo-mon (gate to the palace enclosure), and the Banshonagaya (guardhouse).

Impressive stonewalls reinforcing the steep hill.

Above Layered enclosures carved out of the hill create a *hashigokaku*-style layout, with the Honmaru being at the highest point, followed by the Ninomaru, then the Sannomaru. The Tenshu of Marugame is one of only 12 original Tenshu left today in Japan.

DIRECTIONS
10 minutes walk from Maru-game Station (Yosan Line).

Color key on page 37

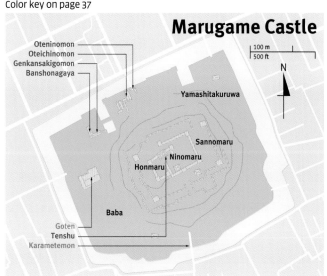

Marugame Castle

Oteninomon
Oteichinomon
Genkansakigomon
Banshonagaya
Yamashitakuruwa
Sannomaru
Ninomaru
Honmaru
Baba
Goten
Tenshu
Karametemon

Location Marugame, Kagawa prefecture
Nickname Kameyama-jo, Horai-jo
Type Hirayamajiro
Layout Hashigokaku
Tenshu type Sotogata, Dokuritsushiki (Independent)
Family crest Ikoma, Yamazaki, Kyogoku

Marugame

Nagoya Castle 1610–1628

Below A male and female *kinshachi*, (golden *shachihoko*) adorn the roof ridge of the Daitenshu. Standing 8.5 ft (2.6 m) high and weighing over 2,646 lb (1,200 kg), these dolphin/tiger ornaments are covered in 18 carat gold.

Nagoya lies on the Tokaido Highway 217 miles (350 km) west of the Tokugawa shogunate's home provinces around Edo and 112 miles (180 km) east of Toyotomi Hideyori's headquarters at Osaka. In 1610, Tokugawa Ieyasu ordered the construction of Nagoya Castle to secure this strategic position and ward off attacks from Osaka. Following the defeat of the western forces loyal to Toyotomi Hideyoshi at the Battle of Sekigahara, *daimyo* on the losing side had their lands confiscated or reduced, resulting in thousands of samurai becoming *ronin*—wandering warriors without a lord or stipend. The displaced *daimyo* and *ronin* mostly lived in the west, ready to support Toyotomi Hideyori if called upon. Thus, while Hideyori was alive and ensconced at Osaka Castle, a constant threat to the Tokugawa leadership remained in the west.

Nagoya Castle was built for Tokugawa Ieyasu's ninth son, Yoshinao, who established the Owari branch of the Tokugawa family. The

Left The seven-story concrete Daitenshu of Nagoya Castle dominates the surrounding area. The original Tenshu of 1612 was destroyed by a US bomb in May 1945. Plans to rebuild the Daitenshu and its connected Kotenshu (small Tenshu) in timber are currently underway, with an estimated completion date of 2026 and a cost of 50 billion yen.

Below center Originally called the Nishinomaru-enokidamon, this two-story tower gate is a 1959 reconstruction of the main gate which burnt down in 1945.

Left The curve in the wall of the Daitenshu base helps distribute the massive weight of the Tenshu over a larger area. Steeply inclined walls were more prone to collapse than fan-shaped ones (*ogikobai*).

Right The Ninomaru-higashishininomon (Ninomaru east second gate). Originally constructed as the east gate of the Ninomarugoten, it was relocated to this site in 1972.

Owari were the foremost of the Tokugawa family's three lineages (*sanke*) and lived here until the Meiji Restoration. Designed by Nakai Masakiyo, who was involved in the construction of Nijo (1603), Fushimi (1602), Edo (1593–1636) and Sumpu (1607) castles, Nagoya was the last castle to be built on the orders of Tokugawa Ieyasu (1542–1616). Nakai combined the latest castle building techniques with the vast resources of 20 *daimyo* to create a massive symbol of Tokugawa power. Incredibly, the castle was completed in two years.

Situated on a flatland site, the castle lacked height and topography for its defense. Significant fortifications were thus built to thwart enemy attacks. The skilled castle engineer Kato Kiyamasa was responsible for the stonewall construction. The walls supporting the Tenshu are called fan walls (*ogikobai*) because the upper part of the wall curves outward like a fan. This specialized technique was used to prevent the wall swelling and collapsing. It is also called Kiyomasa-style Crescent Stonewall after Kato Kiyomasa, who used these sweeping walls at his own castle at Kumamoto.

Left The narrow walkway and small iron door of the Daitenshu were designed to impede an invading army.

Below The original seventeenth-century Tatsumiyagura overlooks the dry Uchibori (inner moat) and protects the southeast corner of the Honmaru. One of three corner towers to survive the bombing during World War II, the others are the Hitsujisaruyagura (southwest tower) and the Inuiyagura (northwest tower).

The cornerstones of the Tenshu base bear the inscriptions of the *daimyo* in charge of construction. Those of Kato and his retainers can be seen on the northeast corner.

A combination of dry and wet moats surround enclosures at Nagoya Castle. The Uchibori, a dry moat, surrounds the Honmaru (inner enclosure) and a wet moat, Sotobori (outer moat), surrounds the castle complex. There are four main enclosures: the Honmaru at the center, the Nishinomaru (western enclosure), the Ninomaru (second enclosure) to the east and the Ofukemaru to the north. The Tenshu and Honmarugoten are located in the Honmaru. A second palace was constructed in the Ninomaru in 1617 for the lord to live in and administer local government. The palace had two Noh drama stages. Performances were held to commemorate a feudal lord's succession to a fiefdom and to celebrate the birth of an heir. In

the early years of the Meiji era, the Ninomaru east garden was leveled and the pond filled in to make way for an army barracks. The castle was finally reopened to the public in 1978.

The massive seven-story, plaster-covered timber Tenshu was connected via a corridor to a smaller Tenshu. At the time of construction, it was the largest Tenshu in Japan, with the biggest floor area. Nagoya Castle relied on its size rather than beauty to impress. Its only concession to decoration are the two huge gilded *shachihoko* on the roof ridges. Clever devices such as hidden shooting holes and stone-throwing windows formed part of the Tenshu's defenses in the case of a siege. Secret storerooms hid rice, money and wells. The Tenshu and Honmarugoten were destroyed in air raids in 1945 and later rebuilt in concrete in 1959. The Honmaru palace is being reconstructed using traditional materials and methods, and is due for completion in 2018.

POINTS OF INTEREST

The *kinshachi*, the golden dolphin tiles on the roof ridge of the main Tenshu. The dolphins are plated in 18 carat gold 0.04 in (0.15 mm) thick. Each is unique. The male is 8.6 ft (2.62 m) high, weighs 2,805 lb (1,272 kg) and has 112 scales. The female is 8.5 ft (2.58 m) high, weighs 2,680 lb (1,215 kg) and has 126 scales.

Family inscriptions (*kuromon*) in the stonewalls. These represent the *daimyo* responsible for a particular section of a stonewall.

The large Kiyomasa stone in the Honmaru was donated by Kato Kiyomasa, the lord of Kumamoto. Known for his skill in building castle walls, Kato was responsible for much of the wall building at Nagoya Castle. It is said he stood on a large rock to direct the selection and placement of individual stones.

The Honmarugoten palace, which is being reconstructed using original drawings, paintings and records.

DIRECTIONS

Subway
Meijo Line, get off at Shyakusho (City Hall).
Tsuramai Line, get off at Sengencho.
Bus
Sakae No. 13, get off at Nagoyajo Seimon Mae.
Key Route Bus No. 2, get off at Shyakusho.
Take a Nagoya Sightseeing Route Bus called Me-guru.
Train
Meitetsu Seto Line, get off at Higashi Ote.

Above A dry moat with walls in *nozurazumi* (rough field stone style) surrounds the Honmaru (inner enclosure). Various kinds of stonewall construction can be seen at Nagoya Castle, the most sophisticated being the Tenshu base and at important gateways.

Right The Omoteshoin (main hall) of the reconstructed Honmarugoten was used for official audiences. The raised floor area through the sliding *fusuma* was reserved for *daimyo* and other important guests. The Honmarugoten was originally built in 1615. A second palace was constructed in the Ninomaru in 1617 where the lord lived and administered local government.

Color key on page 37

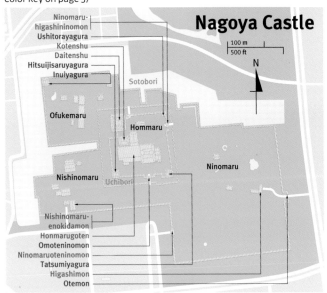

Location Nagoya, Aichi prefecture
Nickname Kinshachi-jo (Golden Shachihoko)
Type Hirajiro
Layout Renkaku
Tenshu type Sotogata, Teiritsushiki (Connected)
Family crest Tokugawa (Owari clan)

Edo Castle 1593–1636

Edo Castle was the headquarters of the Tokugawa shogunate from 1603 to 1868. During the Tokugawa reign, the once backwater fishing village of Edo grew to become one of the most populous and thriving cities in the world, known today as Tokyo. Ota Dokan (1432–86), the chief retainer of the Uesugi clan, built a castle on this site in 1467. It was seized by Hojo Ujitsuna of Odawara in 1524 and held by the Hojo until they were defeated by Toyotomi Hideyoshi in 1590. Hideyoshi then offered Tokugawa Ieyasu the Hojo's eight Kanto provinces in exchange

for the Tokugawa ancestral lands of Mikawa and Totomi. This change in territory shifted Tokugawa Ieyasu, the second most powerful warlord, 149 miles (240 km) east of Toyotomi's power base in the Kinai district. With Tokugawa removed, Toyotomi was able to consolidate the leadership of Japan. Being consigned to a backwater enabled Tokugawa to develop his new territory without being obliged to participate in any of Hideyoshi's costly Korean campaigns. He used this strength to his advantage at the Battle of Sekigahara in 1600, and in his final battles to defeat the

Toyotomi house at Osaka in 1615 and 1616.

Located in the center of Japan on the east coast of the main island of Honshu, Edo lies at the junction of the three main highways of the time: the Tokaido, Nakasendo and Koshi Kaido. Its prime position beside the sea facilitated trade and transport, while the vast Kanto plain around it ensured a good supply of food.

Tokugawa Ieyasu commenced building his castle here in 1593. Appointed shogun by the emperor in 1603, he employed accomplished castle architect Todo Takatora to design a castle fit for the ruler of the country. Drawing upon incumbent *daimyo*, he built a huge castle encircled by a 10 mile (16 km)-long outer moat. A 3 mile (5 km) inner moat fed by the Sumida River protected the inner enclosure of the castle. The grounds were divided into six enclosures: Kitanomaru (north enclosure); Honmaru, which housed the Tenshu and offices of the shogunate; Ninomaru and Sannomaru, which held residences of retainers; Nishinomaru, the living quarters of the past shogun and the heir; and Fukiage, which held gardens. There were 38 gates and numerous towers and bridges. Ieyasu's grandson Iemitsu completed the castle in 1636, the same year Edo was officially made the administrative capital of Japan. Kyoto remained the Imperial capital.

Daimyo were allocated land within the outer moat of Edo Castle to build elaborate mansions in which to reside while on duty at the shogun's court every alternate year under the *sankin kotai* system. Family members were left in Edo as hostages to ensure a *daimyo*'s loyalty. The mansions contained barracks for the *daimyo*'s retainers, homes for clan officials, an audience hall and living quarters of the *daimyo*'s family, fireproof storehouses and beautiful gardens. Lesser vassals of the shogun were assigned areas outside the castle grounds.

Merchants and craftsmen were enticed to Edo by ample business opportunities and moderate taxes. Land to the south and east of the castle was exclusively reserved for them.

Opposite The Fujimiyagura was used as a substitute Tenshu after the main Tenshu was destroyed by fire in 1657. The shogun watched fireworks at Ryogoku and over Tokyo Bay from this tower, and it was also possible to see Mt Fuji from here, hence its name. Situated in the southeastern corner of the Honmaru, it is the only three-story tower remaining of 11 in the inner citadel.

Top The Tenshudai (Tenshu base) is located in the north corner of the Honmaru. It is 135 ft (41 m) wide, 148 ft (45 m) long and 36 ft (11 m) high. A 131 ft (40 m)-high five-story Tenshu stood on this base, making Edo Castle's Tenshu the tallest in Japan at 167 ft (51 m). Built in 1607, the magnificent tower adorned in gold ornaments burnt down just 50 years after completion. With a secure hold on power, there was no immediate need to rebuild and alternative towers in the castle grounds were used as lookouts during the Edo era (1603–1868).

Above The Sakuradamon is located on the southern perimeter of the castle grounds. A *masugatamon* (box-style gate), it is made up of a simple post-and-beam gate, a stonewalled courtyard and a heavily fortified two-story tower gate.

Left The Tatsuminijuyagura (southeast two-story tower) on the Kikyobori (moat) guarded the distant Kikyomon, which led to the Ninomaru.

Above Fushimiyagura was relocated from Fushimi Castle after it was dismantled in the early seventeenth century. The Western-style stone and iron bridge in the foreground replaced the timber Edo-era bridge, Nishinomarushimojobashi, in the Meiji era (1868–1912). This bridge leads to the Nishinomaru where the shogun's living quarters were located and where the Imperial palace stands.

Below The base of the two-story second gate of the Sakuradamon has perfectly cut stones (*kirikomihagi*) of various colors, which fit tightly together without mortar. The most sophisticated and expensive type of stonewall piling, it is seen more frequently at Edo Castle than at any other castle, a result of the Tokugawa making use of the resources of outside *daimyo*.

In 1610, Edo was a thriving town of 150,000 people, and by 1700 it was the largest city in the world, with over a million inhabitants.

In 1867, Tokugawa Yoshinobu, the fifteenth head of the Tokugawa shogunate, handed power back to the Imperial court at Nijo Castle in Kyoto. Edo Castle was occupied by Imperial forces. In 1868, Emperor Meiji moved the Imperial court from Kyoto to Edo Castle and named the new capital Tokyo (eastern capital).

POINTS OF INTEREST

Both stone-faced walls and earth embankments can be seen at Edo Castle. The southern and western sides are fortified by high earth embankments planted with pine trees to prevent erosion. The northern and eastern embankments of the palace grounds are faced with stone. A huge number of stones were shipped from the Kansai and Izu regions. Stones were unloaded on the beach where Tokyo Station now stands and transported to the site by ox or horse.

The stone bases of most of the gates and towers are constructed with precision cut and inserted stone without gaps or the need for mortar (*kirikomihagi*). Extensive use of this expensive type of stone piling was a proclamation of Tokugawa wealth.

The Tenshu of Edo Castle was built on the orders of the second shogun, Hidetada, in 1607. It underwent massive repairs in 1622 before completion in 1638 on the orders of the third shogun, Iemitsu. The five-story, 167 ft (51 m)-high structure, built of *hinoki* (cypress), dominated the city. Unfortunately, only 19 years later, in

1657, the magnificent tower burned down in the Great Fire of Meireki, which razed most of Edo. It was never rebuilt. The Tenshudai (base of the main tower) is located in the north corner of the Honmaru. Rising 36 ft (11 m), it is 134 ft (41 m) wide and 147 ft (45 m) long. The base comprises light-colored stones from Shodo Island in the Seto Inland Sea and dark stones from Izu.

The extensive moat system at Edo Castle covers a total area of 4,304,000 sq ft (400,000 sq m). Made in 13 sections, the moats were on average 4 ft (1.25 m) wide.

Edo Castle during the cherry blossom season.

Color key on page 37

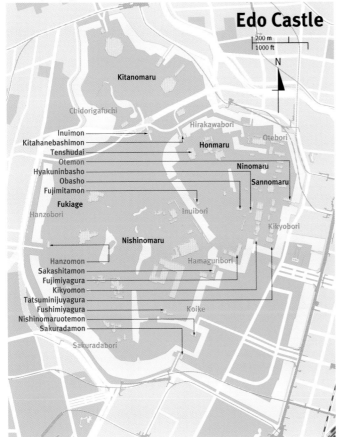

DIRECTIONS
The Otemon entrance to the Kokyo Higashi Gyoen (east gardens) is a short walk from Otemachi Station on the Chiyoda, Tozai, Marunouchi, Hanzomon and Mita Subway Lines. It can also be reached in a 10–15 minute walk from Tokyo Station. The east gardens are on the former site of the Honmaru and Ninomaru.

Location Tokyo, Tokyo prefecture
Site perimeter 10 miles (16 km)
Type Hirajiro
Layout Renkaku
Tenshu type Borogata, Dokuritsushiki (Independent)
Family crest Tokugawa

Maruoka Castle 1576

Problems stabilizing the stonewalls of Maruoka Castle arose during its construction in 1576. It was decided that a human post (*hitobashira*) was needed as a sacrifice to appease the gods. A blind peasant woman called Oshizu agreed to be a *hitobashira* in exchange for her son being taken in by the lord and made a samurai. Oshizu stood still as the stones were laid around her, slowly crushing her to death. The lord, however, never fulfilled his promise

and when the moat floods it is said to be the tears of Oshizu.

Shibata Katsutoyo was the first lord of Maruoka Castle. He was unable to fulfill his promise to Oshizu because he was transferred to Nagahama around 1582. Katsutoyo was the nephew of one of Oda Nobunaga's top vassals, Shibata Katsuie. After Oda was killed in 1582, Shibata Katsuie and Toyotomi Hideyoshi vied for the right to take Oda Nobunaga's place. Toyotomi convinced Katsutoyo to side with him

Above Maruoka Castle is one of the last Late Warring States (1560s–1570s) style of castle before the modern castle was developed during the frenetic castle building period of 1576–1615. The independent timber Tenshu has two levels and a watchtower. Located on a low hill, a high stone base was employed for extra height. Being an earlier castle, techniques of stonewall piling were still in their infancy and rough field stone piling (*nozurazumi*) was used. Unfortunately, this type of stonewall construction is not suitable for a steeply inclined wall, which would account for the instability of Maruoka's Tenshu base.

On the right side of the Tenshu is a timber slatted stone-dropping window (*ishiotoshimado*). These stone-dropping windows are unique to Maruoka Castle. Timber slats enabled defenders to shoot at an enemy, while the floor could be lifted for rocks, hot sand and water to be thrown down on anyone scaling the walls.

Left Access to the Tenshu is via a steep ramp with stone steps.

Left A square shooting hole viewed from inside the Tenshu. In line with Japanese aesthetic ideas of allowing materials to age naturally, the timber has been left raw. However, exposed timber made the castle more susceptible to fire and for this reason later castles usually had their shooting holes plastered.

Below left The round stone roof eave end tile (*nokimarugawara*) is carved with the *tomoe* pattern of three commas. The *tomoe* evokes the image of sprinkling water and often has small dots surrounding the three commas. This pattern is often used on houses to 'protect' the building from fire. The stone roof tiles, stone end tiles and stone *shachihoko* (fish/tiger ornament) are a unique feature of Maruoka Castle.

The Tenshu survived both the Edo and Meiji eras until 1948 when an earthquake leveled the building. In 1955, it was rebuilt using 80 percent of the original materials.

POINTS OF INTEREST

Stone roof tiles made of Shakudani stone and stone *shachihako* (fish/tiger ornament) on the roof.

The castle walls, stone-dropping windows and shooting holes are all made of timber.

Borogata-style viewing platform.

Hitobashira (human post).

DIRECTIONS

From Awara-onsen Station on the Hokuriku Line take the Keifuku bus to Hon-Maruoka and get off at Shiro-iriguchi. Buses run hourly and take 20 minutes. Buses also run hourly from Fukui Station.

against his uncle, and moved him to Hideyoshi's old castle at Nagahama.

Maruoka Castle subsequently had 17 lords rule until the Meiji Restoration. It was nicknamed Kasumiga jo (Mist Castle) because legend says that fog would cloak it in times of war.

Although built in the Momoyama period (1575–1600), the Tenshu is indicative of a fortress from the Warring States period (1477–1575), with a viewing platform on the top floor, thin timber walls and a stone tiled roof. The Tenshu base is quite high and steep and uses random-style stone piling (*nozurazumi*).

Color key on page 37

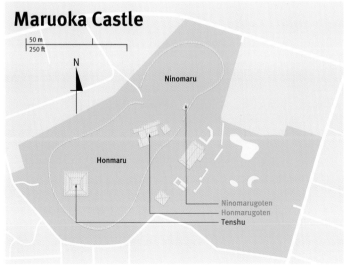

Maruoka Castle

50 m
250 ft

N

Ninomaru

Honmaru

Ninomarugoten
Honmarugoten
Tenshu

Location Maruoka, Fukui prefecture
Nickname Kasumiga-jo (Mist Castle)
Type Hirayamajiro
Layout Renkaku
Tenshu type Dokuritsushiki (Independent)
Family crest Shibata, Aoyama, Honda, Arima

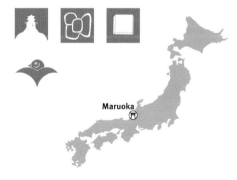

Maruoka

Hirosaki Castle 1603–1611

Some distance from Kyoto, in northern Honshu, lies Hirosaki. Although its location shielded it from the power struggles taking place in central Honshu, the area experienced several years of fighting among local warlords in the last quarter of the sixteenth century. Originally controlled by the Nambu clan, fighting began in 1571 when a member of a subordinate branch of the clan, Oura Tamenobu, revolted. Tamenobu pledged loyalty to Toyotomi Hideyoshi in 1590, who supported him as an independent warlord. Oura subsequently changed his name to Tsugaru Tamenobu. He supported Hideyoshi at the Battle of Odawara in 1590 and participated in the Korean Expedi-

tions. He switched allegiances before the Battle of Sekigahara in 1600, joining forces with the Tokugawa side. For his support, Oura was granted an increase in his territory and given permission to retain Hirosaki. Although beset by a number of disturbances, uprisings and incompetent management, the Tsugaru clan kept their domain throughout the Edo era until the Meiji Restoration in 1868.

Tsugaru began construction on Hirosaki Castle in 1603 but died in 1608 leaving his son Tsugaru Nobuhira to complete it. The five-story Tenshu in the Honmaru burnt down in 1627 after being struck by lightening. In 1810, it was replaced with a three-level Tenshu relocated from the Ninomaru.

The extensive grounds of Hirosaki Castle cover nearly 124 acres (50 ha) and house a number of unique buildings. There are five original *yaguramon* (tower gates), three towers, a Tenshu and a guardhouse. Extensive moats surround the four main enclosures: the Honmaru, Ninomaru, Sannomaru and Nishinomaru. Today, the grounds have been turned into a public park, with the Tenshu housing a museum of samurai artifacts and other items relating to the castle's history.

POINTS OF INTEREST

Hirosaki is one of the best preserved castles in northern Japan. Several important cultural properties date

Top The Higashiuchimon (east gate) guards the entrance to the Ninomaru (second enclosure). The absence of walls on either side suggests times were relatively stable when this gate was built.

Left In a unique procedure called *hikiya*, the 400 ton (406,420 kg) Tenshu was lifted off its base in 2013 to enable renovation works to the stone base and surrounding walls. Twenty-seven jacks elevated the Tenshu 4 in (10 cm), and then over a period of 10 weeks the fully intact building was moved horizontally to the center of the main enclosure 230 ft (70 m) away. It is scheduled to be returned to its original site by 2020.

from 1611: Otemon, Higashimon, Tatsumiyagura, Hitsujisaruyagura, Ushitorayagura, Minamiuchimon, Higashiuchimon, Kitamon, Tenshu and Yorikibansho.

The five tower gates are in a style rarely seen at other castles. The two-story timber *yaguramon* are free-standing and devoid of the usual stone base or adjacent stonewall used for additional strength. Earth embankments with low timber walls create *masugata* box-shaped gateways at the Kitamon (north gate) and Otemon (main gate). Each gate has a small guard window on the lower floor and an extended slatted window on the second floor for samurai to shoot at intruders. The roofs of the gates are steep due to high snowfall.

There are three original towers in the castle grounds. Like the gates, these are in a style not commonly seen at other castles. Three stories high, set on a low stone base on earth embankments, they appear squat compared to the typical two-story castle tower. The white plastered walls are devoid of decoration, as are the three roof layers. The second-story roof has an unusual *irimoya* gable, where the sides extend right to the edge of the roof corners.

The Tenshu in the Honmaru has two different faces. From outside the Honmaru, the Tenshu is well proportioned and graceful. Stone-dropping windows are topped with sweeping gables (*kirizumihafu*) and evenly spaced windows run between white plastered bands. From inside the Honmaru, however, the Tenshu is quite utilitarian, with flat walls, no gables and grouped windows with plain copper shutters.

Above The Otemon (main gate) is a free-standing two-story *yaguramon* guarding the entrance to the Sannomaru (third enclosure). A *masugata* (box-shaped) gateway is created by the timber and plastered mud walls extending from the gate to form a courtyard on the inside of the Otemon. These low timber walls sit atop earth embankments. It is unusual to see earth embankments without stone facing at important gateways.

DIRECTIONS

A 25 minute walk from Hirosaki Station.

Color key on page 37

Hirosaki Castle

100 m
500 ft

N

Nishinomaru

Honmaru

Tenshu
Higashiuchimon
Yorikibansho
Ushitoranoyagura
Kitamon
Hitsujisaruyagura
Minamiuchimon
Tatsumiyagura
Higashimon
Otemon

Sannomaru

Ninomaru

Location Hirosaki, Aomori prefecture
Nickname Takaoka jo
Site area 124 acres (50 ha)
Type Hirayamajiro
Layout Renkaku
Tenshu type Sotogata, Dokuritsushiki (Independent)
Family crest Tsugaru

Hirosaki

Wakayama Castle 1585

After Toyotomi Hideyoshi subjugated Kishu province in 1585, he ordered his younger brother, Hidenaga, to build a castle on Mt Okayama (now known as Mt Torafusu). Todo Takatora oversaw the construction of the castle. Wakayama was the first of many significant castles Todo designed over the next four decades.

Hidenaga was transferred to Koriyama Castle within a year and Kuwayama Shigeharu, a retainer of Toyotomi Hideyoshi, was installed. After the Battle of Sekigahara, Asano Yoshinaga was sent to Wakayama. Asano increased the size of the castle, created the interconnected Tenshu, built a residence in the Ninomaru and changed the main gate from the Okaguchimon to the Ichinohashimon. In 1619, Asano Nagaakira was transferred to Hiroshima Castle and given the eight Bingo provinces stripped from Fukushima Masanori for defying the Tokugawa shogunate.

The Tokugawa shogunate then sent Tokugawa Yorinobu, the tenth son of Tokugawa Ieyasu, to Wakayama Castle. As one of the *sanke* houses (three Tokugawa houses from which the shogun was chosen), Wakayama Castle became the most important fortress to watch over the western provinces. Descendants of the Tokugawa family remained at the castle until the Meiji Restoration. The eighth shogun, Yoshimune, and the fourteenth shogun,

Iemochi, came from Wakayama Castle.

After 1871, when the feudal system was abolished and the country divided into prefectures, the castle became an army lookout. In 1900, it was opened to the public and designated an Historic Site in 1931. Destroyed in an air raid in 1945, it was rebuilt in concrete in 1958.

Wakayama Castle is one of the few castles to have an inner courtyard created by interconnecting towers to a main Tenshu. Himeji Castle is another example. The main three-level Tenshu (Otenshu) is connected to the Kotenshu, a small keep on one side, and to an extended corridor (*gamon*) leading to the Tenshuninomon. This gate is linked to the Ninomonyagura (second gate tower), which is joined by a corridor

to the Inuiyagura, which connects to the Daidokoro kitchen and back to the Kotenshu. Originally, the castle was covered in black timber paneling typical of early castles and those built by supporters of Toyotomi Hideyoshi. In 1798, Tokugawa Harutomi, the tenth lord, ordered the castle's exterior changed to white plaster. This may have been for greater fireproofing or to align it with the other Tokugawa

Below The Otenshu (main keep). On the right is the Kotenshu (small keep) and a single-level corridor leading to the Inuiyagura (not shown). The Inuiyagura was connected by a corridor to the two-level Ninomonyagura. This tower protected the Kusunokimon (gate to the Tenshu). Another corridor connected this gate and the Otenshu, thus creating an enclosed courtyard at the center of the Tenshu complex.

castles, which were usually white. In 1846, the castle was struck by lightning and destroyed. Unlike other castle buildings destroyed during the Edo period that were not rebuilt due to lack of funds, necessity or permission from the shogunate, Wakayama Castle received special permission and was rebuilt in 1850.

POINTS OF INTEREST

Lantern base in the stonewall of the Inuiyagura.

Enormous curved stone-dropping windows.

Closed courtyard created by the connected Tenshu and towers.

Covered corridor gate connecting the Ninomaru and Sannomaru.

Long steps (*gangi*) for soldiers to climb to the top of a wall overlooking the moat quickly and en masse.

Different types of stonewall piling: rough field stone piling (*nozurazumi*), roughly cut and inserted stones (*uchikomihagi*) and precisely cut and fitted stones (*kirikomihagi*). The earliest walls used the roughest piling, later walls *uchikomihagi* and important gateways *kirikomihagi*.

DIRECTIONS

From JR Wakayama Station a bus to Koenmae busstop takes 15 minutes or it takes about 30 minutes to walk.

Opposite above The Ichinohashi (first bridge) and Otemon (front gate) leading to the Ninomaru (second enclosure).

Above left The Ohashiroka (corridor bridge) enabled the lord, his retainers and ladies in waiting to cross between the Ninomaru and Nishinomaru without being seen from the outside. This type of inclined bridge is unusual. It was reconstructed in 2006.

Above center Inside the Ohashiroka.

Above The Okaguchimon was originally used as the main castle gate. During the Asano period, its name was changed to Karametemon (rear gate) and the Ichinohashigomon was used as the front gate. The Okaguchimon was rebuilt by the Tokugawa in 1621 and survived the air raids that destroyed the rest of the castle in 1945. It was designated an Important Cultural Property in 1957.

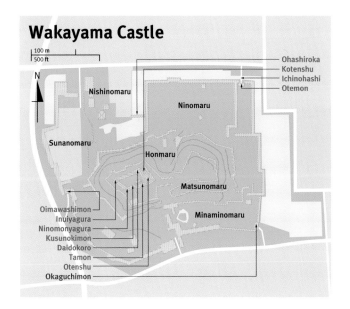

Wakayama Castle

100 m
500 ft

N

Nishinomaru

Ninomaru

Sunanomaru

Honmaru

Matsunomaru

Minaminomaru

Oimawashimon
Inuiyagura
Ninomonyagura
Kusunokimon
Daidokoro
Tamon
Otenshu
Okaguchimon

Ohashiroka
Kotenshu
Ichinohashi
Otemon

Location Wakayama, Wakayama prefecture
Nickname Takegaki, Torafusu
Type Hirayamajiro
Layout Renkaku
Tenshu type Borogata, Renketsushiki (Compound)
Family crest Toyotomi, Kuwayama, Asano, Tokugawa

Wakayama

Fukuyama Castle 1619

By 1616 the Tokugawa had eliminated the Toyotomi house and subjugated the *daimyo* in the western provinces. Most of these *daimyo*, however, had not supported the Tokugawa at the Battle of Sekigahara in 1600 and subsequently sided with the Toyotomi at the sieges of Osaka Castle in 1614 and 1615. The western *daimyo* remained a constant threat to the Tokugawa shogunate throughout the Edo era (1603–1868), and it was pressure from rebellious forces in the west that finally led to the Tokugawa downfall in 1868.

To monitor recalcitrant western *daimyo*, the Tokugawa strengthened existing castles and built new castles at strategic points along the Sanyo

Highway. Himeji Castle was significantly enlarged and strengthened between 1601 and 1617. Mori Terumoto, a Toyotomi loyalist and founder of Hiroshima Castle, 131 miles (210 km) west of Himeji, was removed. Trusted retainers of the Tokugawa shogun were installed at both castles and immediately relieved if their loyalty came into question.

As part of this strategy, the Tokugawa shogunate ordered Mizuno Katsunari to build a castle at Fukuyama, midway between Himeji and Hiroshima, in 1619. Katsunari built a seven-story Tenshu on a small hill. Many buildings were taken from Fushimi Castle near Kyoto and reconstructed, including Fushimi-

Above From the exterior, the Tenshu appears to have five stories but has seven inside. Each floor gets progressively smaller in the *sotogata* style, indicative of *tenshu* built in the latter years of the modern castle building period (1576–1615). The original Tenshu of 1622 burnt down during World War II and was reconstructed in concrete in 1966. It houses the Fukuyama Castle Museum.

yagura, Sujiganegomon, Tsukimi-yagura (moon-viewing tower) and Yudono (bathhouse). Some of them survive in their original condition. Double moats surrounded the castle, fed by an inlet to the Seto Inland Sea.

The Mizuno clan remained at Fukuyama until 1700, after which Matsudaira Tadamasa occupied the castle from 1700 to 1710. The Abe clan followed and ruled the area for the next 164 years.

Left The original Yuudono (bathhouse or hall) was relocated from Fushimi Castle in 1619. It was burnt down during World War II and restored to its original state in 1966. The family crest of Toyotomi Hideyoshi, who built Fushimi Castle in 1594, is carved in the wooden doors.

Right The Fushimiyagura was originally the Matsunomaru higashiyagura of Fushimi Castle. It was dismantled, moved to Fukuyama and renamed in 1619. A two-story turret with a *borogata*-style watchtower, it survived demolition during the Meiji Restoration and the air raids of World War II. It has been designated an Important Cultural Asset.

Left The Tsukimiyagura (moon-viewing tower) is located in the southeastern corner of the Honmaru. Although it is called a moon-viewing tower, it was, in fact, a watchtower. It originally came from Fushimi Castle but was destroyed in the 1870s after the Meiji Restoration. It was reconstructed in concrete in 1966.

Below left More than 10 strips of iron are nailed to the corners of the pillars and doors of the Sujiganegomon. Still in its original state, this gate is believed to have come from Fushimi Castle in 1619. To the left of the gate is a low wall with shooting holes, slatted windows and a tiled roof. Warriors observed and fired on intruders trying to enter the castle from behind these walls.

Below The Yudono bathhouse.

Above The Mizuno family occupied Fukuyama Castle from 1619 to 1700. Their family crest can be seen in the round eave end tiles (*nokimaruguwara*) throughout the castle.

Below The Tenshu is located in the Honmaru at the highest point in the castle grounds. The lower outer enclosures are delineated by stonewalls lined with low plastered mud walls (*dobei*).

Below right Detail of Azuchi-Momoyama style carving in the Karamon at Nishi Honganji Temple, Kyoto. This gate is believed to have come from Fushimi Castle.

Remnants of Fushimi Castle

Fushimi Castle was constructed in 1594 to protect Kyoto from the south and as a place of retirement for Toyotomi Hideyoshi. Located 25 miles (40 km) from Osaka, it was possible to see a fire signal from Toyotomi's main castle at Osaka. Ornate carvings, bright colors and the use of gold leaf were used in abundance in the lavish interiors. The castle is famous for its gold-plated tea room in which Hideyoshi is said to have entertained the emperor. Plum trees were planted at the castle, giving the site the name Momoyama (Plum Mountain). The elaborate style of the Azuchi-Momoyama period (1576–1600) derives its name from Fushimi and Azuchi (1576) castles.

The castle was destroyed in an earthquake in 1595 and another built near the original one. Hideyoshi, however, died soon after its completion.

After Hideyoshi's death in 1598, Fushimi Castle was taken over by Tokugawa Ieyasu before he moved to Osaka Castle the following year. Fushimi Castle was one of the first targets of the Toyotomi loyalists leading up to the Battle of Sekigahara in 1600. Attacked by Kobayakawa Hideaki, it was under siege for 11 days and bravely defended by Torii Mototada before he admitted defeat and committed ritual suicide (*seppuku*). Kobayakawa later sided with Tokugawa Ieyasu at Sekigahara, resulting in the defeat of the Toyotomi loyalists.

In 1602, Tokugawa Ieyasu rebuilt Fushimi Castle but it was dismantled in 1623. Many of its buildings were distributed around Japan, and it is possible to see remnants of Fushimi Castle at Edo Castle, Nijo Castle, Nishi Honganji in Kyoto and Fukuyama Castle.

After the Meiji Restoration, the moats were filled in and many towers were destroyed. The Tenshu and bathhouse were destroyed in World War II air raids, but Fushimayagura and Sujiganegomon survived. Dry stonewalls were later removed to make way for Fukuyama Station, which runs alongside the castle. The Tenshu was rebuilt in concrete in 1966.

POINTS OF INTEREST

The original and unusual Shorou (bell tower).

The four buildings from Fushimi Castle, two of which remain in their original condition.

The reconstructed Yudono bathhouse was originally from Toyotomi Hideyoshi's Fushimi Castle built in 1594. The Toyotomi family crest is carved on the doors of the Yudono.

Above left Steps leading to the area behind Sujiganegomon.

Above Round, square and rectangular shooting holes line the plastered mud walls.

DIRECTIONS

5 minutes walk from JR Fukuyama Station.

Color key on page 37

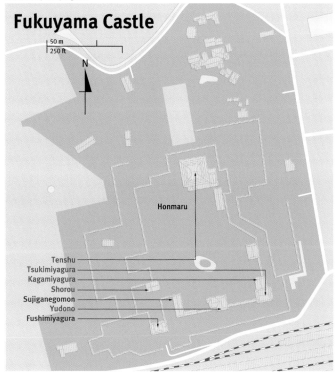

Fukuyama Castle

50 m
250 ft

N

Honmaru

Tenshu
Tsukimiyagura
Kagamiyagura
Shorou
Sujiganegomon
Yudono
Fushimiyagura

Location Fukuyama, Hiroshima prefecture
Nickname Hisamatsu or Iyo Castle
Site area 91 acres (37 ha)
Type Hirayamajiro
Layout Hashigokaku
Tenshu type Borogata, Fukugoshiki (Attached)
Family crest Abe, Matsudaira, Mizuno

Fukuyama

Hagi Castle 1604

L ocated in a remote corner on the west coast of Japan, Hagi Castle was the home of the Mori clan. Prior to the Battle of Sekigahara in 1600, the Mori were one of Japan's wealthiest and most powerful families. As retribution for supporting the losing side at Sekigahara, Tokugawa Ieyasu confiscated six of the Mori's eight provinces, together with their castle at Hiroshima. Ordered to move to Hagi, the Mori's income dropped sharply, from 1.2 million *koku* to 360,000 *koku*.

Having lost territory and most of his income, Mori Terumoto began building a castle at Hagi in 1604. This became the base of the Mori clan for the next 260 years. A school for revolutionary samurai was established here, with most of the graduates playing an important role in overthrowing the Tokugawa shogunate in 1867. In 1863, Mori Takachika moved the administrative functions of the domain to Yamaguchi. Many of the castle buildings at Hagi were dismantled and the castle abandoned in the Meiji era, after 1868.

Hagi is an excellent example of the use of location and topography for defense. The castle town is situated on a pentagonal-shaped island surrounded by the Matsumoto River, the Hashimoto River, the Abu River and the Sea of Japan. A 2,428 ft (740 m)-long outer moat separated the Sannomaru, containing retainer and samurai houses, from the rest of the town where merchants, lower-ranking samurai and artisans lived. The narrow streets of the Sannomaru are lined with plastered mud walls, a timber Nagaya (barracks) and a variety of gates. They were designed to confuse an invading army through sharp turns, dead ends and high walls that obstructed vision. During the Edo era, samurai were permitted to have walls surrounding their house and a front gate befitting their rank. Virtually intact, the town is a remarkable remnant of an Edo-era castle town.

The castle was built on and around Mt Shizuki, a small peninsula extending into the sea. Two enclosures with multiple watchtowers were sited on top of the 470 ft (143 m)- high peak. The Honmaru, Tenshu and administrative buildings were

Top Built in 1845 and originally located in the Sannomaru, the Hananoe tea house was moved to Shizuka Park in 1889. Many political discussions were held here between *daimyo* and vassals in the years leading up to the Meiji Restoration. The southern samurai led by the Mori were to play an important role in overthrowing the Tokugawa shogunate in 1867.

Below A view of the Uchibori (inner moat) from the base of the Tenshu. A five-story, 47 ft (14.4 m)-high Tenshu was located on this base at the foot of Mt Shizuki. Built in 1604, it was the symbol of Hagi Castle for 270 years before being demolished in 1874 after the Meiji Restoration.

Above A long wall of steps (*gangi*) beside the Tenshu enabled warriors to ascend the wall speedily and en masse if attacked.

Above right The Kitanosoumon (north gate). There were three main gates at Hagi Castle: the Kitanosoumon, Nakanosoumon (middle gate) and Hiyakonosoumon (main gate). These gates were closed overnight, prohibiting passage without a permit.

positioned at the base. A moat separated the Ninomaru from the Honmaru. An extensive wall, the Jugan *dobe*i along the seafront, protected the castle from seaborne invasion.

POINTS OF INTEREST

Although there are no extant buildings, the size of the Tenshu base and stonewalls reveal the significant scale of the original castle.

A long wall of stairs (*gangi*) beside the Tenshu base for warriors to ascend quickly.

Enormous rocks with chisel marks in the Tsumenomaru show how rocks were split for building walls and bases.

Samurai houses and mud walls lining the streets in the Sannomaru.

Merchant houses in the castle town.

DIRECTIONS

Although Hagi is remote and takes time to reach, it is well worth the effort. Its location on the coast is stunning, with unspoilt beaches and surrounding mountains. The town is extremely well preserved and the castle ruins extensive. The castle is a 15 minute bus or 10 minute taxi ride from Hagi Station.

Color key on page 37

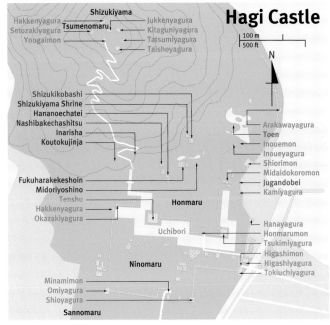

Hagi Castle

Shizukiyama
Hakkenyagura · Jukkenyagura
Setozakiyagura · Tsumenomaru · Kitaguniyagura
Yougaimon · Tatsumiyagura
Taishoyagura

100 m / 500 ft

N

Shizukikobashi
Shizukiyama Shrine
Hananoechatei
Nashibakechashitsu
Inarisha
Koutokujinja

Arakawayagura
Toen
Inouemon
Inoueyagura
Shiorimon
Midaidokoromon
Jugandobei
Kamiyagura

Fukuharakekeshoin
Midoriyoshino
Tensho
Hakkenyagura
Okazakiyagura

Honmaru

Uchibori

Hanayagura
Honmarumon
Tsukimiyagura
Higashimon
Higashiyagura
Tokiuchiyagura

Ninomaru

Minamimon
Omiyagura
Shioyagura

Sannomaru

Location Hagi, Yamaguchi prefecture
Nickname Shizuki-jo
Type Yamajiro and Hirajiro
Layout Hashigokaku
Tenshu type Borogata, Fukugoshiki (Attached)
Family crest Mori

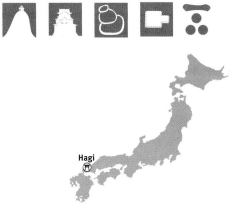

Hagi

Takeda Castle

1441, 1577

Top The Tenshudai (Tenshu base) is located in the Honmaru (central enclosure).

Above Mountain castles were effectively lookouts and only used as a last line of defense. Battles were usually fought on open ground. As Japan unified in the latter quarter of the sixteenth century, *daimyo* needed to be closer to the people to rule efficiently. Castles became an administrative center as well as a fortress. Consequently, the mountain castle was rendered obsolete by the end of the sixteenth century. This view of the town below is from the Ninomaru (second enclosure).

Perched 1,158 ft (353 m) above sea level, Takeda Castle sprawls over the top of the mountain overlooking the surrounding Tajima region in north Hyogo. This site was first used in the mid-fifteenth century when local *daimyo* Sozen Yamana ordered the construction of a castle to protect the Tajima area from warlords in Harima and Tanba. His retainer, Otagaki Mitsukage, built the castle in 1441 and was subsequently made its lord. Originally a simple mountain fort of earthworks and wooden palisades, the top of the mountain

was leveled to permit uninterrupted surveillance of the nearby mountains and adjoining valleys.

Over a century later, in 1577, Toyotomi Hideyoshi seized the castle, placing it under the control of his younger brother, Toyotomi Hidenaga. Toyotomi reinforced the earthworks with stonewalls and stone bases, on top of which a Tenshu and towers were erected. Two lords followed Hidenaga—Kuwayama Shigeharu and the final lord of Takeda Castle, Akamatsu Hirohide. Akamatsu fought on the western side at the Battle of Sekigahara in 1600 but switched sides after the Tokugawa victory. He took part in an attack on Tottori Castle and was accused of setting fire to the town. To atone, he was forced to commit *seppuku*. Takeda Castle was abandoned. Mountain castles were now redundant as fighting between rival warlords had ceased upon the country's unification. These remote sites were also inconvenient as lords needed to be closer to the burgeoning castle towns to effectively administer their domain.

Takeda Castle is divided into four parts: Kitasenjo (north area), Minami-senjo (south area), Hanayashiki (west area) and the central area where the Tenshu was located. All excellent vantage points, these sites contain

Left The tower base in the Minamininomaru (southern second enclosure) is constructed of rough field stone piling (*nozurazumi*).

indication of how the castle once covered the top of the mountain. The stonewalls date from the late sixteenth century after the castle was taken by Toyotomi Hideyoshi. Prior to this, the walls were earthen ramparts.

the Honmaru (main enclosure), Ninomaru (second enclosure), Sannomaru and Minaminomaru (south enclosure). The lord's residence was located at the foot of the mountain, the foundations of which have recently been discovered. The castle,

which is said to appear like a sleeping tiger, is nicknamed Torafusu-jo (Tiger Castle).

POINTS OF INTEREST
The stone bases of towers, stonewalls and the Tenshu provide a good

DIRECTIONS
From the back of Takeda Station the trek up the mountain to the castle site takes about 45 minutes or 15 minutes by taxi or shuttle bus, followed by a 10 minute walk to the entrance.

Color key on page 37

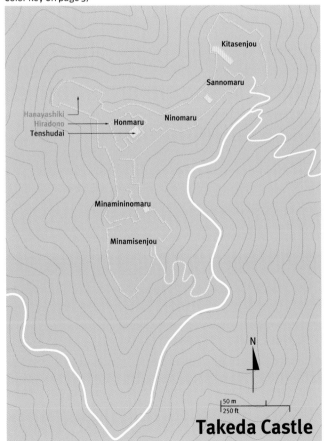

Kitasenjou

Sannomaru

Hanayashiki
Hiradono
Tenshudai

Honmaru   Ninomaru

Minamininomaru

Minamisenjou

N

50 m
250 ft

Takeda Castle

Location Asago, Hyogo prefecture
Nickname Torafusu-jo (Tiger Castle)
Site area 1,312 ft (400 m) north to south, 328 ft (100 m) east to west
Type Yamajiro
Layout Renkaku
Family crest Otagaki, Toyotomi, Akamatsu

Takeda

Fort Goryokaku 1857–1864

Located in Hakodate on the northern island of Hokkaido, Fort Goryokaku was the first Western-style fortress built in Japan. Goryokaku, meaning 'pentagon,' is a five-pointed star-shaped fortress enclosed by a moat. Based on the European fortresses constructed by French military engineer Sebastian Vauban (1633–1707), it was designed by Japanese scientist Ayasburo Takeda in 1857 and completed in 1864. Geometric fortresses were built in this style during the nineteenth century as a defense against modern weaponry.

Lying on a sheltered bay, the city of Hakodate was an international trading port prior to the seventeenth century. It closed after the Tokugawa shogunate ceased all foreign trading, leaving only the southern port of Nagasaki open. Hakodate reopened in 1854 after Commodore Perry demanded

Japan trade with America. The town soon prospered as merchants arrived from the United States, Holland, Portugal, Germany, Switzerland, Denmark, Italy, Austria, Hungary, Spain and Hawaii.

The Tokugawa shogunate ordered the construction of a fort at Hakodate in 1857 as a defense against the threat posed by Russia to the north. The shogunate oversaw the trading activities of Hakodate and the administration of Hokkaido province from within the fort.

Not long after its completion, Fort Goryokaku was tested as a military stronghold when it became the last holdout of the rebel shogunate forces standing against the Japanese Imperial Army. The last battle of the Boshin War (1868–69) was fought here in April 1869. The defeat of the shogunate forces at Goryokaku signaled

the end of feudal Japan and 700 years of samurai rule. The fort was designated a Special Historic Site and is now a public park.

POINTS OF INTEREST

The star-shaped fort is unique in Japan. As the last fort built by the

Below There are three bridges crossing the moat into the inner enclosure: Ichinobashi, Ninobashi and Sannobashi.

Far left The Bugyosho (Magistrates Office).

Left The star shape of the fort is visible from the nearby Goryokaku Tower.

Right Stonewalls line the moat around the inner enclosure.

Tokugawa shogunate, it also marks the site where their rule finally ended.

The former Magistrates Office (Bugyosho) has been reconstructed in the center of the fort. The original building was demolished in 1871.

A bird's-eye view of the fortress is possible from the observation deck of the nearby Goryokaku Tower.

The 1,500 cherry trees planted within the fort grounds make Hakodate a popular spot in spring.

DIRECTIONS

From Hakodate Station, take the tram to Goryokaku Koen Mae, 10 minutes. The fortress is another 10 minutes on foot.

Color key on page 37

Fort Goryokaku

100 m
500 ft

N

Ichinobashi
Bugyosho
Tsuchikura
Itakura
Tsuchikura
Sannobashi
Ninobashi

Hori

Goryokaku
Tower

Location Hakodate, Hokkaido prefecture
Nickname Hisamatsu or Iyo Castle
Site area 92 acres (37 ha)
Type Hirajiro
Family crest Tokugawa

Goryokaku

Japan's **100** Most Important Castles

	Castle Name	City/Prefecture	Date	Type	Historical Significance
1	Akashi	Akashi/Hyogo	1620	Hill	National Historic Site
2	Ako	Ako/Hyogo	1648	Hill	National Historic Site with Important Cultural Properties
3	Akizuki	Akizuki/Fukuoka	1624	Plain	Some original gates remain
4	Azuchi	Azuchi/Shiga	1576	Hill	Important Historic Site, ruins remain
5	Bitchu-Matsuyama	Takahashi/Okayama	1575/1683	Mountain	Important Cultural Property
6	Daishoji	Daishoji/Ishikawa	1575	Mountain	Dry moats and clay walls remain
7	Echizen Ono	Echizen Ono/Fukui	1579	Mountain	Concrete Tenshu
8	Edo	Tokyo/Tokyo	1593–1636	Plain	National Historic Site with Important Cultural Properties
9	Fukui	Fukui/Fukui	1601	Plain	Significant stonewalls, moat and reconstructed bridge
10	Fukuchiyama	Kyoto/Kyoto	1582	Hill	National Historic Site
11	Fukuoka	Fukuoka/Fukuoka	1601	Hill	Important Cultural Property
12	Fukuyama	Fukuyama/Hiroshima	1619	Hill	National Historic Site
13	Fushimi	Kyoto/Kyoto	1594	Plain	Important site, concrete Tenshu
14	Gifu	Gifu/Gifu	1201/1567	Mountain	Concrete Tenshu
15	Goryokaku	Hakodate/Hokkaido	1857–1864	Plain	Special Historic Site, walls and moats remain of star-shaped fort
16	Gujo hachiman	Gujo Hachiman/Gifu	1559	Mountain	Reconstructed Tenshu
17	Hachigata	Yorii/Saitama	1476	Hill	National Historic Site
18	Hagi	Hagi/Yamaguchi	1604	Water	Unesco World Heritage Site, National Historic Site (castle ruins)
19	Hamamatsu	Hamamatsu/Shizuoka	1570	Hill	Reconstructed Tenshu
20	Hikone	Hikone/Shiga	1602–1622	Hill	National Treasure
21	Himeji	Himeji/Hyogo	1580/1601/1617	Hill	Unesco World Heritage Listed, extensive original buildings
22	Hirado	Hirado/Nagasaki	1707	Hill	Reconstructed Tenshu
23	Hirosaki	Hirosaki/Aomori	1603–1611	Plain	Important Cultural Property
24	Hiroshima	Hiroshima/Hiroshima	1589–1599	Plain	National Historic Site
25	Imabari	Imabari/Ehime	1604	Plain	Reconstructed Tenshu
26	Inuyama	Inuyama/Aichi	1535/1601	Hill	National Treasure, original Tenshu
27	Iwakuni	Iwakuni/Yamaguchi	1608	Mountain	Concrete Tenshu
28	Izushi	Izushi/Hyogo	1599	Hill	National Historic Site
29	Kagoshima	Kagoshima/Kagoshima	1613	Hill	Ruins, moat
30	Kakegawa	Kakegawa/Shizuoka	1513/1591	Hill	Local Historic Site, Some original buildings, palace
31	Kakunodate	Kakunodate/Akita	1423/1620	Mountain	Ruins, interesting samurai quarter in town
32	Kameyama	Kameyama/Mie	1535/1590	Hill	Some buildings remain
33	Kanazawa	Kanazawa/Ishikawa	1583–1599	Hill	Important Cultural Property, reconstructed buildings
34	Karatsu	Karatsu/Saga	1608	Hill	Concrete Tenshu
35	Kawagoe	Kawagoe/Saitama	1457	Plain	Palace
36	Kishiwada	Kishiwada/Osaka	1585	Plain	Concrete Tenshu
37	Kiyosu	Kiyosu/Aichi	1427/1478	Plain	Concrete Tenshu
38	Kochi	Kochi/Kochi	1601	Hill	Important Cultural Property, original Tenshu
39	Kokura	Kitakyushu/Fukuoka	1602	Plain	Concrete Tenshu
40	Komoro	Komoro/Nagano	1543	Hill	Stonewalls, moats, significant buildings
41	Komatsu	Komatsu/Ishikawa	1576	Plain	Tenshu base
42	Kubota	Akita/Akita	733/1603	Hill	Reconstructed Tenshu
43	Kumamoto	Kumamoto/Kumamoto	1601	Hill	National Historic Site, significant stonewalls, original buildings
44	Marugame	Marugame/Kagawa	1587	Hill	Important Cultural Property, original Tenshu
45	Maruoka	Sakai/Fukui	1576	Hill	Important Cultural Property, original Tenshu
46	Matsue	Matsue/Shimane	1607–1611	Hill	Important Cultural Property, original Tenshu
47	Matsumae	Matsumae/Hokkaido	1849	Hill	National Historic Site
48	Matsumoto	Matsumoto/Nagano	1590–1614	Plain	National Treasure, original Tenshu
49	Matsushiro	Matsushiro/Nagano	1560	Plain	National Historic Site
50	Iyo-Matsuyama	Matsuyama/Ehime	1602–1627	Hill	Important Cultural Property

	Castle Name	City/Prefecture	Date	Type	Historical Significance
51	Morioka	Morioka/Iwate	1592	Hill	National Historic Site
52	Nagahama	Nagahama/Shiga	1575	Plain	Concrete Tenshu
53	Nagoya	Nagoya/Aichi	1610–1628	Plain	Historic site with Important Cultural Properties
54	Nakagusuku	Futenma/Okinawa	<1450	Hill	Unesco World Heritage Site, Tenshu base and stonewalls
55	Nakajin	Motobu/Okinawa	<1300	Hill	Unesco World Heritage Site, ruins
56	Nakamura	Soma/Fukushima	1611	Hill	Local Historic Site
57	Nakatsu	Nakatsu/Oita	1588	Plain	Concrete Tenshu
58	Nanao	Nanao/Ishikawa	1428	Mountain	National Historic Site
59	Nihonmatsu	Nihonmatsu/Fukushima	1394	Mountain	Stonewalls of significance
60	Nijo	Kyoto/Kyoto	1602	Plain	Unesco World Heritage Listed
61	Obama	Obama/Fukui	1601–1642	Plain	Ruins
62	Odawara	Odawara/Kanagawa	1495	Hill	National Historic Site, concrete Tenshu
63	Ogaki	Ogaki/Gifu	1535	Plain	Concrete Tenshu
64	Oka	Taketa/Oita	1594	Hill	National Historic Site, significant stonewalls
65	Okayama	Okayama/Okayama	1589–1597	Plain	National Historic Site with Important Cultural Properties
66	Okazaki	Okazaki/Aichi	1455	Hill	Concrete Tenshu
67	Osaka	Osaka/Osaka	1583/1620	Plain	Historic site with Important Cultural Properties
68	Ozu	Iyo-Ozu/Ehime	1590	Hill	Local Historic Site with Important Cultural Properties
69	Saga	Saga/Saga	1613	Plain	Local Historic Site with Important Cultural Properties
70	Saiki	Saiki/Oita	1601	Hill	Ruins
71	Sasayama	Sasayama/Hyogo	1609	Hill	National Historic Site
72	Sendai	Sendai/Miyagi	1602	Mountain	National Historic Site
73	Shibata	Shibata/Niigata	1598–1654	Plain	Local Historic Site with Important Cultural Properties
74	Shimabara	Shimabara/Nagasaki	1616	Plain	Concrete Tenshu, impressive stonewalls
75	Shirakawa	Shirakawa/Fukushima	1340/1627	Hill	Local Historic Site with reconstructed Tenshu
76	Shuri	Naha/Okinawa	1200–1300	Hill	Unesco World Heritage Listed
77	Sumpu	Shizuoka/Shizuoka	1585	Plain	Reconstructed buildings
78	Takada	Joetsu/Niigata	1614	Plain	Earthworks instead of stonewalls, reconstructed Tenshu
79	Takamatsu	Takamatsu/Kagawa	1588	Plain	National Historic Site
80	Takaoka	Takaoka/Toyama	1609	Plain	Ruins within a park
81	Takasaki	Takasaki/Gumma	1597	Plain	Local Historic Site
82	Takayama	Takayama/Gifu	1588	Mountain	Ruins
83	Takeda	Wadayama/Hyogo	1441/1577	Mountain	National Historic Site
84	Tanabe	Maizuru/Kyoto	1579	Plain	Some historic buildings
85	Tatsuno	Tatsuno/Hyogo	1499	Mountain	Some historic buildings
86	Tottori	Tottori/Tottori	1532	Mountain	National Historic Site, ruins
87	Tokushima	Tokushima/Tokushima	1586	Hill	National Historic Site
88	Toyama	Toyama/Toyama	1579/1640	Plain	Concrete Tenshu
89	Toyohashi	Toyohashi/Aichi	1505	Plain	Concrete Tenshu
90	Tsu	Tsu/Mie	1571	Plain	Local Historic Site
91	Tsuchiura	Tsuchiura/Ibaraki	1403/1616	Plain	Local Historic Site
92	Tsuwano	Tsuwano/Shimane	1295	Mountain	National Historic Site
93	Ueda	Ueda/Nagano	1583	Plain	National Historic Site
94	Usuki	Usuki/Oita	1653	Hill	Local Historic Site
95	Uwajima	Uwajima/Ehime	1596	Hill	Important Cultural Property
96	Aizu-Wakamatsu	Aizu-Wakamatsu/Fu-kushima	1384	Hill	National Historic Site, concrete Tenshu
97	Wakayama	Wakayama/Wakayama	1585	Hill	National Historic Site with Important Cultural Properties
98	Yamagata	Yamagata/Yamagata	1356/1592	Plain	National Historic Site
99	Yamanaka	Mishima/Shizuoka	1560	Mountain	National Historic Site
100	Yonago	Yonago/Tottori	1602	Hill	National Historic Site

Glossary

Bakufu military government or shogunate

Bansho guardhouse

Borogata type of *tenshu* with a lookout tower

Bushi warrior, samurai

Chidorihafu type of roof gable resembling the outstretched wings of a *chidori* (plover)

Daimyo highest ranking samurai; *daimyo* were lords of a domain or region with an annual income in excess of 10,000 *koku* of rice.

Daitenshu main tower

Degoshimado latticed bay window

Dobei low, plaster-covered earth wall topped with a small tiled roof; set atop stonewalls and interspersed with shooting holes

Domain area of land controlled by a *daimyo*

Dokuritsushiki independent *tenshu*

Doshinen type of castle layout with the main enclosure at the center and the second and third enclosures arranged in concentric rings around it

Dozo storehouse made of timber, mud and straw and covered with plaster

Fukugoshiki attached *tenshu*

Gengyo decoration at the apex of a gable

Gobozumi sophisticated form of random stonewall piling where long rectangular stones were embedded deep into the earth for stability

Goten palace

Hakobori box-shaped moat

Hafu gable

Hashi (*bashi*) bridge

Hashigokaku castle layout, with the main enclosure at the apex of a hill from which the second and third

enclosures descend like steps

Hashira pillar

Hatayagura flag tower

Hei low walls surrounding castle enclosures

Higashi east

Hirajiro castle on a plain

Hirayagura one-level tower

Hirayamajiro castle on a hill surrounded by a plain

Hitsujisaru yagura southwest tower

Honmaru main enclosure/bailey

Hori (*bori*) moat

Idoyagura tower for housing a well

Inuiyagura northwest tower

Irimoya two-sided roof with a closed triangular gable at opposite ends

Irimoyahafu gable in which the two sides extend to the edges of the roof

Ishi stone/rock

Ishiotoshimado stone-dropping window; protruding window with a trapdoor built out over the stonewall for defenders to drop stones, boiling water or oil on attackers scaling the walls

Ishigaki stonewall

-jo suffix meaning castle, Himeji-jo

Kagami enormous stones placed at important entrances

Kanpaku Imperial regent; title given to Toyotomi Hideyoshi who led the country at the end of the sixteenth century.

Karahafu undulating roof gable

Karamete rear gate of a castle

Karamon post-and-beam gate with a cusped gable

Katomado bell-shaped window

Kawara tile

Kirikomihagi cut and inserted

masonry, the most technically advanced form of stone piling; precisely hewn stones were carefully aligned to create a wall without gaps

Kita north

Kotenshu small *tenshu*

Koen park

Koku measurement of rice; one *koku* was considered sufficient to feed a man for a year.

Koraimon post-and-beam gate with a roof extending over the front posts and gate, plus two subsidiary roofs over the rear supports

Kura storehouse

Kuruwa enclosure/bailey (see *maru*)

Mado window

Maru circle, enclosure/bailey (also called *kuruwa*)

Masugatamon series of gates which create a box-shaped defence

Minami south

Mizutemon water gate

Mon gate

Mushamado warrior's window; slatted window through which arrows could be shot

Nagaya tenement house

Namakobei sea cucumber tiling; the kind of tiling used to strengthen plastered mud walls; the rounded, raised plaster between the tiles resemble sea cucumbers

Nawabari layout of the castle

Ninomaru second enclosure

Ninomon second gate

Nijuyagura two-level tower

Nishinomaru west enclosure

Nokimarugawara round eave end tiles which usually displayed the crest of the lord of the castle

Nokihiragawara decorative flat tile lining the roof edge

between the round eave end tiles

Nozurazumi random kind of stonewall piling using field stones (see *ransekizumi*)

Nunozumi type of stonewall piling in which the stones are precisely squared and fitted in even rows

Oginokobai fan-shaped stonewalls

Ohiroma audience hall

Onigawara gargoyle-like 'monster' tiles on the eave corners

Otemon main gate

Ransekizumi type of random stone piling, also called *nozurazumi* or field stone piling

Renkaku castle layout with the main enclosure in the center with the second and third enclosures on either side

Renketsushiki compound *tenshu*

Renjimado push out timber window

Sama shooting hole for archers, gunners or spearmen

Sannomaru third enclosure

Sanjuyagura three-level tower

Sangizumi zipper-like arrangement of rectangular stones at the corners of stonewalls

Shachihoko mythical dolphin-like creatures on the apex of roof gables

Shiro castle

Shogun military leader; the most powerful *daimyo*

Seiren reception rooms

Sotogata multilevel style of *tenshu* where each floor has the same shape but decreases in size toward the top

Sumiyagura corner tower

Taiko retired regent

Taikobei drum wall where the sides bulge out like a drum

Taikoyagura signal drum tower

Tamonyagura extended one-story tower

Tatsumiyagura southeast tower

Teien garden

Teiritsushiki connected *tenshu*

Tenno heavenly sovereign or emperor; the Imperial leader of Japan

Tenshu main castle tower; *donjon*

Tenshudai earth-filled stone faced base of the *tenshu*

Tepposama gun shooting hole

Teppoyagura gun tower

Tsukimiyagura moon-viewing tower

Tsujibei soil wall

Uchikomihagi most common type of piling using individual rocks roughly hewn into shape by hammer and chisel

Ukishiro castle surrounded by water; 'floating castle'

Ushitorayagura northeast tower

Uzumimon small opening in a stonewall

Watariyagura crossing or connecting tower Nishi west

Yagenbori U-shaped moat

Yagura tower or turret; arrow storehouse

Yaguramon two-story tower gate with an opening on the ground floor and guardhouse with firing positions on the first floor

Yakuimon simple gate with a single roof covering

Yamajiro mountain castle

Yamazama arrow shooting hole

Yashiki mansion

Photo Credits All photos by David Green except the following

Published by Tuttle Publishing, an imprint of Periplus
Editions (HK) Ltd

www.tuttlepublishing.com

ISBN: 978-4-8053-1387-9

Distributed by

North America, Latin America & Europe
Tuttle Publishing
364 Innovation Drive
North Clarendon, VT 05759-9436 U.S.A.
Tel: 1 (802) 773-8930
Fax: 1 (802) 773-6993
info@tuttlepublishing.com
www.tuttlepublishing.com

Japan
Tuttle Publishing
Yaekari Building, 3rd Floor
5-4-12 Osaki
Shinagawa-ku
Tokyo 141-0032
Tel: (81) 3 5437-0171
Fax: (81) 3 5437-0755
sales@tuttle.co.jp
www.tuttle.co.jp

Asia Pacific
Berkeley Books Pte. Ltd.
61 Tai Seng Avenue, #02-12
Singapore 534167
Tel: (65) 6280-1330
Fax: (65) 6280-6290
inquiries@periplus.com.sg
www.periplus.com

20 19 18   10 9 8 7 6 5 4 3 2 1

Printed in China   1804RR

About Tuttle
"Books to Span the East and West"

Our core mission at Tuttle Publishing is to create books which
bring people together one page at a time. Tuttle was founded in
1832 in the small New England town of Rutland, Vermont (USA).
Our fundamental values remain as strong today as they were
then—to publish best-in-class books informing the English-
speaking world about the countries and peoples of Asia. The world
has become a smaller place today and Asia's economic, cultural
and political influence has expanded, yet the need for meaningful
dialogue and information about this diverse region has never been
greater. Since 1948, Tuttle has been a leader in publishing books on
the cultures, arts, cuisines, languages and literatures of Asia. Our
authors and photographers have won numerous awards and Tuttle
has published thousands of books on subjects ranging from martial
arts to paper crafts. We welcome you to explore the wealth of
information available on Asia at **www.tuttlepublishing.com.**